taken
for
granted

taken for granted

the remarkable power of the unremarkable

eviatar zerubavel

Princeton University Press   Princeton and Oxford

Published by Princeton University Press
41 William Street, Princeton, New Jersey 08540

In the United Kingdom: Princeton University Press
6 Oxford Street, Woodstock, Oxfordshire OX20 1TR

press.princeton.edu

Jacket design by Chris Ferrante

Library of Congress Control Number 2017959001
ISBN 978-0-691-17736-6

British Library Cataloging-in-Publication Data is available

This book has been composed in Adobe Text Pro
and Helvetica Neue LT Std

Printed on acid-free paper. ∞

Printed in the United States of America

10 9 8 7 6 5 4 3 2 1

[T]he familiar . . . is made "strange" in order that it can be systematically analysed and explored. Hence taken-for-granted assumptions . . . are subjected to a sociological gaze . . . where familiar understandings of social life are challenged.

—**Amanda Coffey,** *Reconceptualizing Social Policy*, **21**

Contents

Preface

Ever since first reading Benjamin Lee Whorf in 1971,[1] I have been fascinated with the relation between language, thinking, and culture. When I applied to graduate school later that year, I even listed "sociology of language" as my main area of interest. Yet only in the early 1980s, while working on my book *The Seven-Day Circle: The History and Meaning of the Week*, did I first explicitly focus my scholarly gaze on the semiotic act of marking, using the distinction between what I came to identify as "marked" and "unmarked" days to capture the pronounced asymmetry between the sacred Sabbath and the six so-called "profane days" of the traditional Jewish week, as well as between the two-day "weekend" and the five "weekdays" in its modern secular form.[2] Later, however, while working on *Time Maps: Collective Memory and the Social Shape of the Past*, effectively inspired by the work of my wife Yael Zerubavel,[3] I further realized that such distinction between "special" and "ordinary" time periods actually captures the very essence of the fundamental difference between not only Sundays and Wednesdays but also the parts of the past we conventionally consider memorable and those we collectively forget.[4] As so vividly evidenced in our history textbooks as well as annual holiday cycles, the underlying structure of our collective memory basically boils down to the fundamental distinction between the culturally marked and unmarked parts of our shared past.[5]

My growing interest in this seemingly ubiquitous cultural distinction between the special and the ordinary soon became one of the staples of my "Cognitive Sociology" seminar, as also evidenced by the work later done by some of my students (Johanna Foster, Jamie Mullaney, and especially Wayne Brekhus) on markedness and unmarkedness.[6] In fact, it even led me to begin my book *Social Mindscapes: An Invitation to Cognitive Sociology* with the question "Why does adding cheese make a hamburger a *cheeseburger* whereas adding ketchup does not make it a *ketchupburger*"?[7] Furthermore, while writing *Ancestors and Relatives: Genealogy, Identity, and Community*, I also became aware of the major role that marking plays in the cultural construction of ethnoracial identity, and even opened the book by asking why we consider Barack Obama a black man whose mother was white rather than a white man whose father was black.[8]

My original plan for this book was to examine the three sibling notions of unmarkedness, backgroundness, and taken-for-grantedness, but I soon gave up on the idea and decided to split this project into two separate books. And only in 2014, indeed, after having completed writing *Hidden in Plain Sight: The Social Structure of Irrelevance*, which focuses specifically on the notion of the "background,"[9] did I finally feel fully ready to begin working on a book dealing exclusively with unmarkedness and taken-for-grantedness.

Fairly early in the process of writing the book I had already identified the pronounced semiotic asymmetry between the marked and the unmarked as perhaps its most important underlying theme. But as I was writing about it I also started to notice a rather disturbing new asymmetry within my very own body. In February 2016 I was in fact formally diagnosed with Parkinson's disease, which soon led me to become aware of yet a further irony. Not only did I notice a progressive decline in the functioning of my right limbs, I also began to realize that I could no longer take hitherto simple motor tasks such as swallowing, buttoning, or typing for granted, which was particularly ironic given that I was in the middle of writing a book about the phenomenon of taking for granted! While having to deal with both the physical and psychological challenges of learning to live with my new predicament, I was therefore nevertheless also gaining a new, effectively experiential perspective on the traditionally strictly theoretical themes about which I was writing.

I should add here, however, that, especially given its very topic, I made considerable efforts while writing the book to avoid as much as possible taking my own default assumptions for granted. Yet despite all those efforts I finally realized that there is simply no way that, as a white, male, straight, middle-class baby boomer, my own outlook on the world can ever be absolutely free of certain fundamental cultural biases that, like many other white, male, straight, middle-class baby boomers, I habitually take for granted, yet that many other people might not.

Several colleagues, students, and friends played a critical role in my efforts to produce this book. I am especially indebted in this regard to Asia Friedman, Stephanie Peña-Alves, and Ara Francis, whose indispensable advice helped me tremendously in bringing it to look the way it does. I am also particularly grateful to Wayne Brekhus, whose own work on markedness and unmarkedness I consider the most ambitious effort yet to explore their social foundations, as well as to Tom DeGloma, Brittany Battle, Barbara Katz Rothman, Judy Gerson, Richard Williams, Johanna Foster, Debby Carr, Alexandra Gervis, Lynn Chancer, Rachel Brekhus, Lisa Campion, Christine Galotti,

Jamie Mullaney, John Levi Martin, Hana Wirth-Nesher, Catherine Lee, Allan Horwitz, Yaacov Yadgar, Viviana Zelizer, Iddo Tavory, and Terence McDonnell, who read early versions of the manuscript and provided me with excellent feedback.

Special thanks also go to Ilanit Palmon for contributing the illustrations for the book, Linda Truilo for copyediting the manuscript, Alan Prince for providing various clarifications regarding language, and Jennifer Waller for giving me some very useful bibliographical tips. And I am particularly grateful to Meagan Levinson for inviting me to publish the book with Princeton University Press as well as for her terrific editorial comments and suggestions. Her great enthusiasm was a tremendous boost during the final stages of completing the book.

Last but not least, endless thanks to my wife, Yael, my daughter, Noga, and my son, Noam. Not only did they read various earlier versions of the book and spent many hours discussing it with me, they also continue to provide me with the great psychological support I so much need as I enter this new non-taken-for-granted stage of my life.

East Brunswick, New Jersey,
August 2017

taken
for
granted

1

The Marked and the Unmarked

The unmarked . . . carries the meaning that *goes without saying*— what you think of when you're *not thinking anything special*.

—Deborah Tannen, "Marked Women, Unmarked Men"

When telling people that he was studying suburban gays, writes Wayne Brekhus, "I was often asked if I am gay. No one ever asked, however, if I was suburban,"[1] thereby tacitly revealing the far greater cultural salience conventionally attached to certain aspects of one's identity than others.

Yet why, indeed, is being gay conventionally considered more culturally salient for determining "what" one is than being suburban? Furthermore, why is the term *openly gay* used far more widely than its nominally equivalent lexical counterpart *openly straight*?

Answering such questions calls for a thorough examination of the concepts of *markedness* and *unmarkedness*.

As their etymology implies, the distinction between the "marked" and the "unmarked" is essentially the distinction between the *remarkable* and the *unremarkable*. In sharp contrast to the former, which figuratively "stands out," the latter is viewed as lacking any distinctive features and, as such, is considered "nondescript." The distinction thus captures the supposedly fundamental difference between "holy" places (a shrine), "formal" attire (a tuxedo), or "festive" food (a birthday cake) and their effectively "mundane" cultural counterparts. As further exemplified by the difference between the occurrences we deem "uneventful" and those we consider "news," it is basically a distinction between the *ordinary*, or "plain," and the *special*.

In sharp contrast to the marked, which is explicitly *accentuated*, the unmarked remains *unarticulated*.[2] As such, it is exemplified by the default options on a computer menu. Reflecting what we *assume by default*, it is thus effectively *taken for granted*.

The distinction between the marked and the unmarked dates back to a 1930 letter from Nikolai Trubetzkoy to fellow linguist Roman Jakobson pointing to the fundamental contrast between pairs of phonemes, one of which possesses a certain feature that the other does not.[3] Naming the one possessing that feature the marked member of the pair and the one implicitly defined by its absence the unmarked one,[4] Jakobson immediately took Trubetzkoy's observation one step further, noting that "*every* single constituent of *any* linguistic system" is in fact "built on . . . the presence of an attribute ('markedness') in contraposition to its absence ('unmarkedness')."[5]

Furthermore, Jakobson also realized that the fundamental distinction between markedness and unmarkedness actually transcends linguistics, indeed noting its overall *cultural* significance,[6] but it took another half-century before it was explicitly incorporated into a somewhat broader *semiotic* framework—a critical intellectual leap made by his student and collaborator Linda Waugh. Concluding her 1982 article "Marked and Unmarked: A Choice between Unequals in Semiotic Structure" with a special section explicitly titled "Examples from Other Semiotic Systems" featuring culturally salient contrastive semiotic pairs such as blackness/whiteness and homosexuality/

heterosexuality,[7] Waugh thus proposed a full-fledged semiotic theory of markedness and unmarkedness.

The act of *marking* sets the special apart from the ordinary either physically (putting a "One Way" traffic sign to mentally separate a given street from "ordinary," two-way ones), ritually (making a toast on "special" occasions), or institutionally (formally rewarding "exemplary" behavior or an "outstanding" accomplishment). Yet it is most spectacularly exemplified lexically.

After all, the all-too-common dismissive expression "It's just semantics" notwithstanding, *language* certainly reflects the way we think about things, as the actual words we use often reveal our *cognitive defaults*.[8] The term *menstrual cycle*, for example, clearly reveals the considerably greater significance culturally attached to the menstrual phase of women's hormonal cycle than to its reproductively far-more-critical yet nevertheless semiotically unmarked ovulatory counterpart.[9] By the same token, consider the term *white trash*, which to this day "still flies with little self-conscious hesitancy on the part of the user [and] continues to be sustained socially by an almost unconscious naturalness."[10] Although originally designed to mark poor whites who do not conform to their expected and thus unmarked middle-class racial image and are therefore considered "not quite white,"[11] in fact it actually marks not only "white *trash*" but also "*white* trash"! After all, as an adjective, it is indeed the word *white* that is ultimately designed to modify the default meaning of the noun *trash* rather than the other way around, and the term *white trash* thus actually marks not only white people who are considered "trashy" but also "trashy" people who happen to be white. If they were black, or so goes this essentially racist default assumption, the term *black trash*, for example, would have been considered redundant.

That certainly exemplifies the important role of *labeling*, the most effective form of marking, in establishing and maintaining the fundamental cultural contrast between what we explicitly mark and what we implicitly assume by default and take for granted. Given the existence of the Black Entertainment Television cable network and the Women's National Basketball Association, for example, the very absence of a "*White* Entertainment Television" network and an explicitly gendered "*Men's* National Basketball Association" thus underscores the fact that whereas blackness and femaleness are conventionally marked in America, whiteness and maleness are not. By the same token, given the presence of "Arab Affairs" newspaper, radio, and television correspondents in Israel, the glaring absence of "Jewish Affairs" journalists likewise implies that, in sharp contrast to Arabness, Jewishness is conventionally considered ordinary there. In a similar vein, in sharp contrast to its lexical counterpart *male nurse*, the term *female nurse* is conventionally considered redundant, "for saying *nurse* already implies that."[12]

The extent to which something is conventionally considered ordinary, in other words, is inversely related to the availability of cultural labels to denote it. The taken-for-grantedness of the unmarked is thereby evidenced in its *semiotic superfluity*, as manifested in the paucity of cultural labels denoting what is conventionally assumed by default. Being regarded as literally un-remarkable, it is not considered worth mentioning.

It would therefore be useful to compare the actual vocabularies culturally available for denoting marked versus unmarked phenomena in a given speech community. As we shall see, the relation between such vocabularies is indeed pronouncedly *asymmetrical*, with terms denoting marked phenomena being much more widely available than ones denoting their unmarked counterparts.

Thus, for example, given the historical closetedness of homosexuality in America, one would expect the term *openly gay* to be far more widely used there than its nominally equivalent counterpart *openly straight*. By the same token, the term *working mom* reflects the traditionally marked status of middle-class working mothers, which sharply contrasts with the effectively unmarked status of working fathers. Conventionally assumed by default and thus taken for granted, the latter thereby require no special marking, and a term such as *working dad*, for instance, would actually seem redundant.

Along similar lines, we thus also "have the *career woman* . . . but not the career man. Men by definition have careers, but women who do so must be marked. . . . A man can also be a *family man*, but it would be odd to call a woman a *family woman*. Women are by definition family women."[13] Indeed, by lexically marking traditionally "special" people (male nurses, the openly gay, middle-class working moms), we tacitly also characterize their "ordinary," unmarked counterparts by the very absence of presumed and thereby seemingly superfluous adjectival qualifiers such as *female* (for nurses), *openly* (for straights), and *working* (for dads) to denote them.[14]

Such pronounced cultural asymmetries can in fact be demonstrated empirically by measuring actual lexical usage through frequency counts of the words and phrases people use, with glaring statistical gaps between nominally equivalent lexical pairs exemplifying the fundamental *semiotic asymmetry* between the marked and the unmarked. Whereas a simple Google search for the term *openly gay*, for example, yields 3,740,000 hits, a parallel search for its nominally equivalent counterpart *openly straight* yields only 32,800.[15] While the former denotes what is conventionally deemed "special" and therefore literally remark-able, the latter denotes an "ordinary," culturally unremark-able phenomenon conventionally assumed by default and thereby taken for granted.

In a similar vein, whereas a search for the term *working mom*, for example, yields 8,520,000 hits, a parallel search for its nominally equivalent lexical counterpart *working dad* yields only 117,000.[16] And while a search for the term *first-generation students* yields 282,000 entries, a parallel search for its nominally equivalent counterpart *third-generation students* yields only 6,880.[17] Similar searches yield significantly more results for *abnormal psychology* (3,290,000) and *seafood* (174,000,000) than for their respective nominally equivalent lexical counterparts *normal psychology* (37,600) and *landfood* (25,900).[18]

Effectively exemplifying the pronouncedly asymmetrical amounts of cultural attention respectively paid to the marked and the unmarked, frequency counts of the actual words and phrases people use thus represent *collective attention* patterns.[19] And indeed, whereas the marked is by its very definition highly noticeable and thereby culturally "visible," the unmarked represents the "background" regions of our phenomenal world,[20] which typically escape our attention.[21] It is in fact its cultural *invisibility*, therefore, that so distinctly characterizes the unmarked.

Whether one considers something marked or unmarked is by no means just a matter of personal opinion. Yet nor is anything *inherently* marked or unmarked. Specialness and ordinariness are in fact but *social* constructions, products of particular *semiotic norms, traditions,* and *conventions* that we share as members of specific "thought communities."[22] And as we shall see, what we assume by default and therefore take for granted indeed varies across cultures as well as among different subcultures and across different social situations within a given society.

As we mark things, thus effectively implying that they cannot be assumed by default and therefore taken for granted, we actually "abnormalize" them, thereby tacitly also *normalizing* what remains unmarked. Marking (and thereby abnormalizing) femaleness, blackness, homosexuality, or disability, for example, is thus effectively inseparable from the conventional semiotic tradition of presuming the normality of maleness, whiteness, straightness, and able-bodiedness.

As we shall see, normality plays a major role in establishing as well as maintaining social dominance, which in fact involves the power to affect what others come to take for granted by tacitly leading them to make certain default assumptions without their even realizing that they are making them! Such dominance is manifested in the power to actually set the very standards of normality as well as to abnormalize, through a politico-semiotic process of "othering," whatever deviates from them. Indeed, it is the fact that they are conventionally considered "self-evident" and thereby assumed by default and taken for granted that allows certain ideas, practices, and identities to maintain their cultural dominance.

In fact, the more dominant a social group, the more likely is its identity to remain unmarked. It is thus socially dominant identities such as maleness, whiteness, straightness, and able-bodiedness that are conventionally assumed by default and taken for granted, and their bearers who therefore often become culturally invisible.

A full-fledged *sociology of markedness and unmarkedness*[23] thus reveals the way in which structures of power are socially produced, maintained, as well as reproduced. But as we shall see, in so doing it also helps reveal the ways in which those very structures are sometimes challenged and subverted.

The present book is an attempt to draw explicit attention to what we implicitly assume by default and therefore take for granted. Yet how, indeed, are we to actually "take account of . . . the banal, the quotidian, the obvious, the common, the ordinary . . . the background noise, the habitual?"[24]

Anybody who ventures to study the taken-for-granted inevitably faces a formidable epistemic challenge. After all, as we are reminded by Friedrich Nietzsche, "what we are used to is most difficult . . . to see" as an actual object of inquiry.[25] The unmarked regions of our phenomenal world are therefore "elusive and slippery things, providing . . . no outside perspective or scaffolding" on which to figuratively stand.[26] Indeed, it actually took social anthropologists Daniel Miller and Sophie Woodward six months of studying the cultural practice of wearing blue jeans to realize that those pants' most significant property is in fact their ordinariness:

> While it was always obvious that denim could be described as ordinary, the suggestion that this might be the key to our findings didn't occur to us . . . until around six months into our fieldwork. . . . Initially the word *ordinary* seemed so banal, more a taken-for-granted background than a pretender to the crown of accomplished research. For the same reason, arriving at a sense of the profundity and importance of ordinariness took even longer.[27]

As a result, the unmarked has rarely been studied per se,[28] thereby still remaining an intellectual blind spot.[29] Despite the many studies involving heterosexual sex, for example, heterosexuality itself has until relatively recently been assumed by default and thus taken for granted, thereby effectively escaping analysis.[30] The same, indeed, has been true of maleness, whiteness, and able-bodiedness.

Furthermore, given the fact that the unmarked distinctly lacks certain properties characteristically possessed by the marked,[31] studying it thus also involves the epistemic challenge of having to observe *absence*, thereby making it methodologically elusive. Acts of omission, after all, are much harder to notice than acts of commission (which is why neglected children are often unaware of what they are *not* getting), and whereas the disabled often provide vivid accounts of the challenges they face, the experience of being able-bodied is not so readily articulable.[32]

Exploring the very phenomenon of unmarkedness thus requires the ability to actually notice what is "conspicuous by its absence" and thereby "see" and "hear" the conventionally invisible and inaudible. And given the fact that the unmarked is effectively inarticulable, exploring it requires being particularly attentive to what linguists call *lexical gaps*. As we encounter the terms *male nurse*, *working mom*, and *openly gay*, for example, we thus need to be able to also "hear" the absence of their nominally equivalent counterparts—*female nurse*, *working dad*, and *openly straight*.

Studying the unmarked, in short, requires exceptional self-reflectiveness about what we habitually and thus pre-reflectively take for granted![33] Given such a formidable methodological challenge, the paucity of actual studies of taken-for-grantedness therefore comes as no surprise.[34] Such studies, however, nonetheless promise us "a startling new view of a previously invisible, taken-for-granted, 'normal' . . . universe."[35] And in so doing they may therefore "unsettle forever" our very idea of normality.[36]

2

Semiotic Asymmetry

The social marking process is metaphorically illustrated in Nathaniel Hawthorne's *Scarlet Letter* [wherein] Hester Prynne's community literally marks her with a scarlet letter "A" [that] symbolizes her identity as an "adulteress" and sets her apart from the unmarked category of "marital loyalists." In a similar fashion, Nazi Germany used pink triangles to accent the identity of "homosexuals" as distinct from the unmarked category of "heterosexuals." . . . [Yet] Germany did not require "heterosexuals" to wear a different colored triangle, nor did Prynne's neighbors wear an "ML" to signify their identity as "marital loyalists." These categories were defined in default by their absence of any mark.

—Wayne Brekhus, "Social Marking and the Mental Coloring of Identity," 500

The main purpose of marking is the establishment of a fundamental semiotic asymmetry between "marked" and "unmarked." Such asymmetry is manifested, for example, in the pronouncedly uneven semiotization of streets that are specifically marked with "Do Not Enter" signs and ones that are *not* marked with "Please Enter" ones, food products that are explicitly labeled "organic" and ones that have *no* labels specifically marking them as tainted by the use of pesticides, and explicitly marked bike lanes and ones that are *not* specifically designated "car lanes." By the same token, in stark contrast to parking spots and public-restroom stalls specifically designed for people with disability, there are none specifically designed for the able-bodied. Like the term *openly straight*, the latter member of each of these nominally symmetrical semiotic pairs is assumed by default and therefore taken for granted. As such, unlike its nominally equivalent counterpart, it is effectively considered semiotically superfluous.

As one might expect, having established such fundamental semiotic nonequivalences, many of the distinctions we make between otherwise seemingly symmetrical conceptual pairs ("right" and "left,"[1] "life" and "death," "healthy" and "sick") are therefore effectively lopsided. And it is precisely such pronounced asymmetry that most distinctly characterizes the relation between the marked and unmarked regions of our phenomenal world.[2]

That, of course, is a result of the fact that the contrast between the two ultimately boils down to a fundamental asymmetry between the highly pronounced presence of certain features in marked semiotic objects and the equally pronounced absence of those features from their nominally equivalent unmarked counterparts.[3] That is why we have, for example, "wheelchair-accessible" doors and buildings yet no specifically designated "foot-accessible" ones, special "quiet" cars on trains yet no explicitly marked "noisy" ones. By the same token, while there is a special road sign indicating a curvy road ahead, there is no such sign similarly indicating a straight one. And whereas Google searches for the terms *bisexual* and *biracial* yield 153,000,000 and 6,350,000 results respectively, parallel searches for their nominally equivalent counterparts *monosexual* and *monoracial* yield only 65,300 and 42,300 (not to mention that my word-processor's automatic spell-checker immediately flags them as typos, thereby tacitly exemplifying their semiotic superfluity).[4]

Such asymmetries, of course, reflect the pronouncedly uneven distribution of cultural attention we respectively pay to the marked and unmarked regions of our phenomenal world. And since the former are culturally attended to significantly more than the latter, they also come to carry much greater "weight."

Semiotic Weight

Tacitly invoking the image of a tilted scale in an effort to capture the very essence of semiotic asymmetry, it was sociologist
Jamie Mullaney who first called attention to the pronouncedly
lopsided distribution of *semiotic weight* we respectively attach
to culturally marked and unmarked human behavior.[5] After
all, as so evocatively exemplified by the fundamental cultural
asymmetry between kissing someone on the lips and "only"
on the cheek (and thereby respectively signifying romantic versus "merely" platonic relations),[6] marked acts clearly
"count"[7] more (that is, are more "weighty" and thus culturally significant) than unmarked ones. By the same token, the
nominally equivalent acts of drinking a bottle of whisky and a
bottle of water are nevertheless respectively associated with
marked, noun-like ("a heavy *drinker*") and unmarked, verb-
like ("he *drank* it in one gulp") identities,[8] with the former,
supposedly signifying what people "are" rather than just what
they "do," effectively carrying much greater identity-salient
"weight" than the latter.[9] As so aptly captured by the collo-
quial notion of "losing" one's virginity, one's very first sexual
intercourse, for example, is thus conventionally regarded
as actually affecting one's very essence far more than one's
seven-hundred-and-fifty-eighth one.[10] And whereas a single
marked act such as murdering someone is considered highly
salient for identity attribution, even four thousand instances
of unmarked ones such as raising one's eyebrows or wiping
one's nose are not. In sharp contrast to being identified as a
murderer, after all, no one is ever identified as an "eyebrow
raiser" or a "nose wiper."[11]

The way we respectively define femininity and masculinity
further exemplifies the pronouncedly asymmetrical distribution

of semiotic weight between marked and unmarked identities. Women's clothing, for example, is far more gendered (and therefore culturally marked) than men's clothing, and women who wear pants today clearly do not jeopardize their perceived femininity to the same extent that men who wear dresses might jeopardize their perceived masculinity.[12]

In a similar vein, consider also the highly uneven cultural salience conventionally attached in America to "white" and "nonwhite" ethnoracial identities. Americans are thus much more likely to be cognizant of the Puerto Rican (or at least "Hispanic") roots of Jennifer Lopez or Ricky Martin, for example, than of the Finnish roots of Jessica Lange or Matt Damon. And as so poignantly exemplified by the infamous "one-drop rule" (whether in its traditional legal or modern informal form), whereas blackness implies the genealogical presence of relatively recent African ancestors (lest one forget, we *all* descend from *non*-recent ones), whiteness implies their genealogical absence rather than the presence of European ones.[13] Thus, whereas having even a single recent African ancestor often suffices to establish one's blackness, having several European ancestors may not always suffice to establish one's whiteness. In short, while African and European ancestors are effectively equivalent in terms of what they actually contribute to their descendants' genetic makeup, they nevertheless differ considerably in their respective semiotic contributions to their racial identity, since descending from the former is conventionally considered much weightier than descending from the latter (which is why Barack Obama, for example, is usually considered a black man whose mother was white rather than a white man whose father was black).

The basic logic underlying such *"one-drop"* semiotics also helps account for the inclusion of the letter "B," which stands

for *bisexuality,* in the acronym "LGBT." As we shall see, semiotically speaking, homosexuality "weighs" far more than
heterosexuality. As a result, despite the fact that bisexuality is
actually a blend of both homo- and heterosexual tendencies,
bisexual individuals tend to be lumped with homosexual rather
than heterosexual ones. The homosexual component of one's
bisexual identity, in other words, thus clearly "counts" far more,
and is therefore culturally weightier, than its nominally equivalent yet evidently "lighter" counterpart.

Tacit Assumptions and Cognitive Defaults

When something is taken for granted, it is effectively considered *self-evident,* or axiomatic.[14] As such, it actually remains
unquestioned[15] and therefore also undisputed.[16] What we take
for granted, in short, is basically taken as a "given."[17]

The act of taking something for granted, given its fundamentally pre-reflective nature,[18] is ultimately done habitually[19]
and therefore pretty much automatically. The essence of the
unmarked is thus best captured by the notion of *default,* which
basically implies the idea of *tacit, implicit assumptions* that remain in effect until explicitly overridden.[20] Unless something
is specifically marked, in other words, we therefore tend to
assume by default that it is unmarked. Thus, unless we have
reason to suspect that new people we meet might actually be
illiterate, disabled, or mentally ill, for example, we usually give
them the benefit of doubt, thereby *presuming* them to be liter-
ate, able-bodied, as well as mentally healthy, that is, bearers of
unmarked identities normally assumed by default.

One of the distinctive features of the things we take for
granted is the fact that they do not need to be explicitly artic-

ulated. In other words, they "go without saying."[21] Since they are essentially presumed, they are considered semiotically superfluous. Given the conventional assumptions that nurses are female and that male adults work, for example, the terms *female nurse* and *working dad*, as we saw, are indeed culturally redundant. By the same token, given the fact that romantic relationships are conventionally presumed to be monogamous, it is hardly surprising that whereas a Google search for the term *polyamory* yields 2,230,000 results, a parallel search for its nominally equivalent yet effectively assumed-by-default and therefore conventionally taken-for-granted counterpart, *monoamory,* yields only 2,490.[22]

By tacitly revealing what we habitually and therefore automatically take for granted, unmarkedness thus provides a lot of information about our cognitive defaults (such as our basic assumptions that nurses are typically female, that male adults usually work, and that romantic relationships tend to be monogamous). Markedness, by contrast, implies an explicit deviation from such defaults.[23]

In order to be able to assume something by default and thereby take it for granted we first need to consider it "ordinary" rather than "special." After all, the assurance that what we are about to deal with is in no way "out of the ordinary"[24] provides us with some measure of predictability, thereby effectively making it easier for us to develop some expectations[25] on which we can then base some tacit assumptions. Such sense of presumed ordinariness is therefore disrupted, of course, whenever we encounter the unexpected.[26] Since people are conventionally presumed to be straight, for example, we are far more likely to be surprised to learn that somebody is gay than to find out that he is actually straight, which is what we had assumed by default and therefore taken for granted, after all. Learning that someone's identity is unmarked, in other words, does not surprise us because it does not disrupt any prior expectations we had and therefore also any prior assumptions we might have tacitly made.

As a result, while unmarkedness is implicitly taken for granted, markedness actually needs to be explicitly accounted for. Whereas greeting an acquaintance (let alone a friend), for instance, requires no special explanation, failing to do so normally does.[27]

That explains the pronouncedly asymmetrical manner in which we respectively manage information about our marked and unmarked identities. Since the latter (being sighted or having a home, for example) are typically assumed by default and therefore "go without saying," their bearers can normally expect their ordinariness to be taken for granted. Bearers of marked identities (such as being blind or homeless), on the other hand, are actually expected to "announce" their specialness.

Sharing personal information about oneself is thus organized according to its degree of markedness, and items that simply confirm default assumptions are indeed rarely considered "notifiable."[28] Whereas gays and lesbians, for example, often feel compelled to "come out," straights, by contrast, are rarely expected to "announce" their sexual orientation (which, after all, is conventionally presumed). By the same token, unlike vegetarians and vegans, nor are other dinner guests expected to proactively notify their hosts in advance that they *do* eat meat.

By the same token, since it is conventionally presumed that one is *not* terminally ill, one is rarely expected to simply volunteer such noninformation, although it is certainly tacitly assumed by one's family and close friends, for example, that one would actually notify them if one *is* indeed terminally ill. Claiming later that they did not explicitly ask one about that or that the subject simply "never came up" is unlikely to be accepted as a legitimate account for one's failure to proactively "announce" one's markedness.

Consider, for example, in this regard the scene from the film *The Crying Game* in which Fergus discovers to his great horror that Dil, the woman with whom he is about to go to bed, is actually a man, or the following exchange in *School Ties* right after David's hitherto "unannounced" Jewishness, an exceptionally marked feature at an exclusively Christian prep school, is suddenly revealed:

CHRIS: "What do you expect me to say?"
DAVID: "That it's no big deal."
CHRIS: "If it's no big deal, why didn't you just tell me in the first place? I am your roommate."
DAVID: "You never told me what religion *you* are."
CHRIS: "I'm Methodist."
DAVID (*sarcastically*): "You're Methodist, and all the time I didn't know it!"
CHRIS: "That's different."

The difference, of course, lies in our pronouncedly asymmetrical implicit expectations regarding the notifiability of people's marked and unmarked identities. Whereas the latter (being Christian in an exclusively Christian prep school, or a woman if one is dressed and behaves as one) are presumed and therefore do not need to be specifically accounted for, the former (being Jewish in that same school, or a transwoman), by contrast, are by no means taken for granted. And as such, they are conventionally expected to be properly "announced."

The Common and the Exceptional

The fundamental asymmetry between the marked and the unmarked is also manifested in the pronouncedly uneven manner in which the referential scopes of marked and unmarked terms are respectively delineated. As so starkly exemplified by contrasting *front door* with *door*, *volleyball* with *ball*, *ethnic food* with *food*, or *women's literature* with *literature*, the former tend to be more specific (that is, more narrowly delineated) and therefore more semantically exclusive than the latter, which, being less semantically restrictive, tend to have an inherently wider denotative potential.[29]

By the same token, whereas marked terms such as *short*, *young*, *narrow*, and *shallow* have a single, unambiguously specific meaning, their unmarked counterparts (*tall*, *old*, *wide*, and *deep*) can actually assume a specific as well as a generic meaning. Such nominally equivalent lexical pairs, after all, "are not completely symmetric. . . . [I]f one asks *How tall is Harry*? one is not suggesting that Harry is tall, but if one asks *How short is Harry*? one is suggesting that Harry is short."[30] In other words, *tall* can be used more specifically, as in *He is very tall*, thereby excluding *short*, as well as more generically, as in *How tall is he*? thereby also including it.[31] And in a similar vein, in sharp contrast to its nominally equivalent marked counterpart *night*, the term *day* can actually be used to refer not only to a specific part of a twenty-four-hour period, as in *he works during the day and sleeps at night*, but also to that entire period, as in *it rained for three straight days*.

As one might expect given their broader referential scope, unmarked terms also tend to be more widely distributed.[32] After all, being less semantically determinate than their marked counterparts, they can also be used in a wider range of contexts.

Terms "that have a relatively focused and specific meaning will tend to be used in narrowly defined ways," whereas ones "that have relatively less focused and more generic meanings will have a wider range of uses . . . resulting in their broader distribution."[33] *Markedness is thus inversely related to statistical prominence*, as what we choose to mark tends to be proportionally smaller than what remains unmarked.[34]

I have thus far defined markedness and unmarkedness in strictly experiential terms, yet marked semiotic objects actually "stand out" not only experientially but also statistically. We therefore need to characterize the unmarked and the marked not only as ordinary and special but also as *common* (that is, usual or typical) and *exceptional* (that is, unusual or atypical).

As exemplified by our tendency to mark that which is less frequently encountered,[35] it is the statistically aberrant that usually draws our semiotic attention. A widely used term, after all, implies that, perhaps counterintuitively, the phenomenon it denotes is culturally atypical. Had it been more commonly encountered, we would have most likely taken it for granted and not felt the need to explicitly label it. We thus use the terms *male nurse, working mom,* and *openly gay,* for example, much more frequently than their nominally equivalent counterparts *female nurse, working dad,* and *openly straight* precisely because the cultural phenomena they denote have traditionally not been as commonly encountered as being a female nurse, a working dad, or openly straight.

Such a specifically statistical conceptualization of markedness and unmarkedness also allows for a better understanding of the way we conventionally view normality. Indeed, as Emile Durkheim, effectively equating the normal with "the most frequently occurring," put it, the statistical prominence of a phenomenon ought to be considered the very "criterion of

[its] normality."[36] That would in fact explain, for example, why we conventionally regard wearing eyeglasses (in sharp contrast to using a wheelchair) as "normal" rather than as a generally accepted mark of "disability."

Theorizing markedness as an essentially statistical phenomenon also helps us realize that nothing is inherently marked or unmarked, let alone "normal." And it is to such a pronouncedly social constructionist critique of the very notions of markedness and unmarkedness that we now turn.

3

Social Variations on a Theme

After all, being ordinary might be represented by bright yellow if everyone else is wearing it.

—Daniel Miller and Sophie Woodward, *Blue Jeans*, 115

Marking Traditions

What we mark as well as leave unmarked may vary from one individual to another, as evidenced by the contrasting manner in which different people tend to envision the proverbial glass as half-empty or half-full or view the world as fundamentally dangerous or safe. As exemplified by the ultimately pessimistic habit of vigilantly waiting for the figurative "other shoe" to drop, some people, for instance, adopt an effectively cautious approach, essentially presuming that things are dangerous unless actually proven safe. Operating on such fundamental default assumption, argues Ruth Simpson, they specifically mark "safe" persons, objects, places, and activities while taking potentially "dangerous" ones as a given. Others, by contrast, adopt a diametrically opposite, trusting approach, effectively presuming that things are safe unless actually proven dangerous. Assuming safety by default, they specifically mark "dangerous" persons, objects, places, and activities while considering "safe" ones a given.[1] The difference between those two fundamentally contrasting approaches, of course, lies in what each one's users specifically mark and what they take for granted and thereby leave unmarked.

Yet while our tendency to make either of those default assumptions is partly personal, it is by no means strictly so. After all, it is in our specific capacity as socially trained and formally licensed drivers, for example, that we *learn to assume* safe road conditions unless we encounter special road signs ("Falling Rocks," "Sharp Curve Ahead," "Deer Crossing") specifically warning us about potential hazards.[2] Such learning is part of our *semiotic socialization,* thereby reminding us that we actually set our cognitive defaults *not only as individuals but also as social beings.*

The act of taking something for granted, in other words, "has its origin *beyond the individual,* and it is this sociocultural basis that forms the interpretive background of our individual minds."[3] What may seem at first glance to be a strictly personal act ultimately explainable in terms of individuals' personal tendencies thus turns out to actually be a product of essentially *impersonal,*[4] non-idiosyncratically patterned default assumptions that are not unique to particular individuals.

In fact, we often *share those assumptions with others* as parts of an intersubjective and therefore social reality to which we have been semiotically socialized, thereby presuming that others take for granted what we do.[5] As exemplified by the special Kosher labels used to mark grocery food products that do not present a potential danger for observant Jews who follow the strict dietary laws of kashrut, the assumption that things are fundamentally dangerous unless specifically designated safe is often a *collective* one. Thus, when Woody Allen told his audience, "My mother used to say to me when I was younger, 'If a strange man comes up to you, and offers you candy, and wants you to get into the back of his car with him . . . *go*'" and they found it funny,[6] it was because they shared the common presumption that children actually ought to stay away from such tempting yet potentially dangerous situations.

To further appreciate the way we are sometimes actively *socialized to presume* that things are fundamentally dangerous and that we therefore need to be particularly vigilant, consider also "defensive driving" courses specifically designed to train motorists to proactively anticipate potentially hazardous situations, or the special classes people need to take in order to obtain a gun-carry permit. Such classes, reports author Dan Baum, are essentially

> about recruiting us into *a culture animated by fear* of violent crime. . . . [W]e watched lurid films of men in ski masks breaking into homes occupied by terrified women. We studied color police photos of a man slashed open with a knife. Teachers in both classes directed us to websites [in which] the gun-carrying community warns, over and over, that crime is "out of control."[7]

> [G]un carriers are evangelizing a social philosophy. Belief in rising crime . . . amounts to faith in a natural order of predators and prey.[8]

In other words, it is in their specific capacity as members of "the gun-carrying community," and thereby having been socialized into (and thus internalized) its collective default worldview, that gun carriers, like formally certified "defensive drivers," learn to view the world as fundamentally dangerous and thereby consider safety the exception rather than the rule.[9]

The semiotic socialization of concealed gun carriers and "defensive drivers" underscores the pronouncedly impersonal "styles" of marking we come to share as members of particular *semiotic communities*. They usually take the form of specific *marking traditions*, such as envisioning epidemics in terms of mortality rather than survival rates,[10] presenting labor statistics in terms of unemployment rather than employment rates, featuring ground meat (by contrast to, say, milk or yogurt) as being 96% lean rather than as containing 4% fat, attaching greater weight to the nonwhite ancestors of "multiracial" Americans than to their white ones,[11] or, for that matter, considering the act of communicating with invisible entities normal (and, as such, unmarked) in the case of "God" yet delusional (and therefore effectively marked) in the case of "ghosts."

Marking Conventions

Given its impersonal, let alone collective, nature, one might get the impression that markedness is actually an inherent property of the semiotic objects with which it is commonly associated and that, as such, it is universally attached to them.[12] By the same token, when taking the unmarked for granted, we tend to presume that it is also assumed by default and taken as a given by everyone else.

And yet, in reality, *nothing is inherently marked or unmarked*.[13] Both markedness and unmarkedness, indeed, are but products of specific and therefore nonuniversal *marking conventions*, which vary across cultures as well as among different subcultures and across different social situations within the same society. And it is precisely such variability that attests to their *conventional* and therefore fundamentally social nature.[14]

Given all this, the idea that marking patterns are fundamentally personal is clearly not the only illusion we need to abandon.

It is just as important, in fact, to also give up the diametrically opposite illusion that they must therefore be universal.[15]

For starters, cultures may vary in what their members come to take for granted. Although many languages, for example, consider masculine the default gender, not all actually do.[16] By the same token, while Costa Ricans and New Zealanders are likely to assume peace by default, Afghans and Iraqis are far more likely to define it only residually, as the absence of war. And whereas Cameroonian children are effectively socialized to assume that strangers are fundamentally "safe," German children are not.[17]

Cultures also differ from one another in the default assumptions underlying juridical traditions such as whether defendants are presumed innocent unless proven guilty, and it is the prosecution who therefore bears the burden of proving their guilt, or presumptively guilty, and it is the defense who therefore needs to prove their innocence. Whereas American defamation laws, for instance, stipulate that the burden of proof rests upon the plaintiff, their British counterparts put it on the defendant, so that libelous or slanderous statements are presumed to be false unless the defendant can prove their truth.

By the same token, when visiting a foreign country, one may often not be able to tell whether smoking is permitted anywhere unless there is a sign indicating that it is prohibited, or only in places specifically marked as designated smoking areas. Nor, for that matter, can one know for certain whether to presume beaches to be public unless there are special signs indicating that they are private, or private unless there are signs specifically marking them as public.

As exemplified by what we choose to display in our museums, cultures vary in what they consider "special." And as one might expect, such variability often reflects contrasting statistical realities. Whereas in Yemen and Saudi Arabia, for example, the sight of a veiled woman passes as ordinary, in Uruguay or Lithuania, by contrast, it is highly unusual and therefore effectively marked. By the same token, whereas Joe Lieberman's 2000 nomination for vice-president was marked by many Americans as a historic first, the notion of a Jewish president is actually considered by Israelis a given. And unlike in Austria and Finland, it is actually the use of silverware rather than chopsticks that is marked in Japan and Korea as special.

In a similar vein, whereas in America the far less common non-free-choice form of marriage is specifically labeled *arranged*, in India it is the standard practice and thereby assumed by default, and it is actually unarranged marriage, therefore, that is specifically dubbed there as *love marriage*. It is likewise vegetarianism that is often assumed there by default, and meat-based dishes that are thus residually referred to as *non-vegetarian*.

Situational Variability

Yet what we assume by default and thereby take for granted varies not only cross-culturally but also subculturally. After all, while people often take able-bodiedness for granted, first responders, for instance, rarely do. And as Durkheim famously proposed, in "a community of saints . . . crime as such will be unknown, but faults that appear venial to the ordinary person will arouse the same scandal as does normal crime in ordinary consciences."[18]

By the same token, it is ethnicity- as well as class-based conventions, for example, that affect whether corporal punishment of children is considered ordinary or special, and regional ones that account for why armadillos, which are considered little more than roadkill in the Southwest, are nevertheless specifically showcased in East Coast zoos.[19] And even within the same city the most special day of the week (its "peak," so to speak)[20] may very well be Saturday for Jews, Sunday for Christians, Friday for Muslims, and Monday for those who work on the weekend and take it as their regular day off.[21]

What we actively mark or tacitly take for granted thereby leaving unmarked also varies across different social situations. Thus, whereas shouting back at a preacher would constitute a most unusual and therefore highly marked event at a Catholic service, for example, it is actually considered quite normal in many black churches.[22] By the same token, while remaining silent during a chamber-music concert is in fact expected and, as such, taken for granted, during a job interview or cross-examination it would most likely be considered rather odd and therefore highly marked.

The same semiotic object thus often carries different weight in different situations. A woman who attracts no special attention as a pre-school teacher or beautician, for instance, would most likely stand out at a construction site or coal mine, just as a young boy is much more likely to self-identify as white if he attends an ethnoracially diverse rather than an all-white school.[23] And an ordinary backpack that is unlikely to draw any special attention at a small college library might actually cause great alarm if left unattended at a busy train station.

In fact, there are various situations in which the common designation of something or someone as marked or unmarked is effectively reversed. Whereas being sick, for example, is conventionally considered a marked identity and being healthy an unmarked one, in hospitals it is actually the former that is taken for granted and the latter that would most likely be considered marked. By the same token, whereas "[i]n the unmarked context of an everyday occasion, formal wear is marked and casual clothes unmarked . . . in the marked context of a festive occasion, the markedness values of formal and casual clothes are reversed."[24] And in places "where everyone else is striving to be in fashion and wears brands or designer clothing, *not* wearing brands or fashion" may very well turn out to be the most effective way of dressing "extraordinarily."[25]

Marking Battles

The nonuniversal, effectively conventional nature of marked-ness is also evidenced by the fact that it is often contested, as exemplified by various *semiotic battles* over competing and often conflicting notions of what ought to be marked and what should remain unmarked. The dispute over whether to fund only students whose academic performance is exceptionally strong or any student whose performance is not exceptionally weak, as well as differences over whether the term *terrorist attack* ought to refer only to acts perpetrated by foreign attackers or also include those perpetrated by "homegrown" ones are some classic examples of such battles. So, indeed, is the debate over the very use of the terms *reverse racism* and *reverse discrimination*. While some people argue that the terms *racism* and *discrimination* by themselves cannot be used to denote acts committed by nonwhites against whites and therefore should also include the adjective *reverse*, others insist that they most certainly can, and that the latter is therefore effectively redundant.

Consider also the terms *ordinary Americans* and *everyday Americans*. Since they are effectively vague, one can of course use them as highly inclusionary signifiers of unmarked Americanness, which is indeed the way they are often used by politicians who try to appeal to a maximum number of potential supporters.[26] At the same time, however, they may actually signify not only unmarked averageness but also marked mediocrity. As columnist Frank Bruni in fact mocked then-presidential candidate Hillary Clinton's use of the term *everyday Americans*,[27]

> is "everyday" a signifier that a voter really craves and feels complimented by? Is it the ideal epithet? You, kind sir, are utterly unexceptional and thus have my devotion. You, dear madam, recede into the cornfields, unnoticed and unnoticeable, but I will find and meet you among the stalks.[28]

As exemplified by the debate over the use of the terms *reverse racism* and *reverse discrimination*, however, of particular political significance are the cultural battles over whether to use the *specific* (and therefore marked) or the *generic* (and thus unmarked) forms of culturally "sensitive" semiotic objects. Disputes over whether to name politically "progressive" academic departments "*Women's* Studies" or simply "*Gender* Studies," and their heads *chairwoman* or simply *chairperson* or *chair*, are some classic examples of such battles. So, for that matter, is the annual heated debate over whether to use the effectively Christian-specific (and therefore semantically more exclusive) greeting *Merry Christmas* or its generic (and thereby semantically more inclusive) counterpart *Happy Holidays*.[29] Semantic exclusivity and inclusivity, of course, also signify social exclusivity and inclusivity, the latter greeting thereby representing a conscious effort to be more socially inclusive.

Another classic example of such cultural battles between marked specificity and unmarked genericity is the heated debate between advocates of the explicitly particularistic slogan *Black Lives Matter* and its purportedly universalistic

counterpart *All Lives Matter*, which is in effect a battle between *"Marked* Lives Matter" and *"Both Marked and Unmarked* Lives Matter."[30] Rejecting the seemingly inclusionary
veneer of the counter-slogan *All Lives Matter*, members of the
Black Lives Matter movement keep pointing to the fact that
African Americans are disproportionately targeted as well as
actually killed by the police. As philosopher Judith Butler, for
example, has put it,

> When some people rejoin with "All Lives Matter" they mis-
> understand the problem. . . . It is true that all lives matter,
> but . . . *not all lives are understood to matter* which is pre-
> cisely why it is most important to *name the lives that have
> not mattered, and are struggling to matter*. . . . If we jump
> too quickly to the universal formulation "all lives matter,"
> then we miss the fact that black people have not yet been
> included in the idea of "all lives." . . . ['T']o make that universal
> formulation . . . one that truly extends to all people, we have
> *to foreground those lives that are not mattering now, to mark
> that exclusion*, and militate against it.[31]

Such explicitly anti-generic argument has likewise been voiced
by political activist Donna Brazile:

> Of course ALL lives matter. But there is no serious question
> about the value of the life of a young white girl or boy. Sadly,
> there is a serious question . . . about the value of the life of a
> young black girl or boy. So those who are experiencing the
> pain and trauma of the black experience in this country don't
> want their rallying cry to be watered down with a *generic*
> feel-good catchphrase.[32]

Adopting an explicitly pro-specific stance, she then added,
quoting political commentator Van Jones: "When you have a

specific pain, you want a *specific* slogan,"[33] that is, a specifically marked one.

The semiotic battles over *reverse discrimination, Women's Studies, Merry Christmas,* and *Black Lives Matter* offer us a glimpse into the considerable political implications of both markedness and unmarkedness. And it is to this critical relation between semiotics and politics that we now turn.

4

The Politics of Normality

In any dyadic relationship . . . [i]f the parties are equal in power, we see them as equally different from each other. When the parties are in a relationship of domination and subordination we tend to say that *the dominant is normal, and the subordinate is different from normal*.

—Mari Matsuda, "Voices of America," 1361

As we saw earlier, what we mark tends to be proportionally smaller than what we leave unmarked. Yet as exemplified by the fact that women, who are at least as statistically prominent as men,[1] are nevertheless conventionally marked (and thereby symbolically "minoritized") to a much greater extent, the relation between semiotics and statistics is considerably more complex.

Indeed, unmarkedness is a function of not only statistical (and therefore experiential) prominence but also social *dominance*. At least in formally egalitarian social systems, the more dominant a group, the more its identity tends to remain unmarked[2] and thereby assumed by default and taken for granted.[3]

Having thus far discussed markedness and unmarkedness in strictly experiential and statistical terms, let us now also examine their *political* underpinnings. As we shall see, semiotic asymmetry is often a product of the differential distribution of *power* between marked and unmarked social groups. While marked identities carry greater semiotic weight, it is nevertheless the unmarked ones that tend to carry greater political weight.

Studying the way political *inequality* and social *privilege* are semiotically produced, maintained, and reproduced calls for considering not only semantics (the branch of semiotics that deals with the relations between signs and their meanings) and syntactics (the one that deals with the relations among the various signs within any given semiotic system), but also pragmatics, the branch of semiotics that deals with the way signs are actually used in practice.[4] In other words, it calls for examining not only the respective logics of markedness and unmarkedness but also the actual mechanics of the process of marking.

Consider, for example, the politico-semiotics of gender. After all, one of the most striking, albeit deceptively elusive, manifestations of men's social dominance over women is the taken-for-grantedness of maleness, as embodied in the conventional tendency to regard it as more "basic" than femaleness[5] and thereby assume that *a person is presumably male unless specifically designated otherwise*[6]—a default assumption aptly identified by Hildegard Keller as *andronormativity*.[7] Such a pronouncedly asymmetrical cognitive bias explains, for example, why ungendered fictional characters are often presumed to be male.[8] It also underlies Rudyard Kipling's otherwise odd characterization of San Francisco as a city inhabited "by perfectly insane *people whose women* are of a remarkable beauty"[9]—a statement exemplifying the way in which even a gender-neutral term such as *people* may actually be used specifically to denote men.

Such glaring asymmetry also characterizes the way we think about ethnicity, and especially its particular form we call "race."[10] Thus, for example, in white-dominated societies, whiteness tends to remain unmarked[11] and therefore be taken for granted. In such societies it is therefore conventionally assumed that *a person is presumably white unless specifically designated otherwise*[12]—a default assumption I identify, using the Greek word for "white," as *leukonormativity*.

By the same token, consider also the conventional tacit assumption, famously dubbed by Michael Warner as *heteronormativity*,[13] that *a person is presumably straight unless specifically designated otherwise*. The fact that straightness is conventionally assumed by default, and therefore taken for granted,[14] explains, for example, why male teenagers are often asked whether they already have a girlfriend, and female ones whether they already have a boyfriend.

Consider also, along these lines, the conventional default assumption, identified by Wayne Morris as *able-bodied normativity*,[15] that *a person is presumably able-bodied unless specifically designated otherwise*. Indeed, it is often only the presence of a guide dog, a hearing aid, or a wheelchair ramp that reminds us not to take able-bodiedness as a given.

Effectively taking maleness, whiteness, straightness, and able-bodiedness for granted, these are the cultural default assumptions underlying the pronouncedly asymmetrical manner in which we conventionally envision the glaringly different definitions of identity involved in being male and female, white and nonwhite, straight and gay, and able-bodied and disabled. In examining them, I specifically emphasize their common characteristics in a self-conscious effort to identify the formal, transcontextual features of unmarkedness. Rather than focus on the distinctive features of maleness, whiteness, straightness, or able-bodiedness, I therefore refer to gender, race, sexual orientation, and physical ability almost interchangeably.[16] After all, as essentially analogous cultural default assumptions distinctly associated with unmarkedness,[17] andronormativity, leukonormativity, heteronormativity, and able-bodied normativity all embody our taken-for-granted expectations regarding what we conventionally consider "normal."

Normality and Deviance

Needless to say, the very terms *andronormativity, leukonormativity, heteronormativity,* and *able-bodied normativity* underscore the critical role of *normality* in the process of taking for granted.

Strictly statistically speaking, "normal" is what characterizes the entirety, or at least a majority, of a given population. Yet as Somerset Maugham once quipped, it can also be "the rarest thing in the world."[18] After all, "commonly held ideas about 'normal people' with 'normal families' do not reflect a statistical middle. Instead, *'normal' is a moral and political category* that serves to elevate some families and delegitimize others."[19] Indeed, rather than normality being defined by how statistically prominent something is, it is the fact that it is considered normal that actually makes it statistically prominent!

In other words, rather than being simply a statistical matter, normality is often determined culturally. By the same token, as we shall see, *abnormality* or "aberration" too implies more than just strictly statistical out-of-the-ordinariness.

It may be useful to consider in this regard the notion of *deviance*, which, despite their obvious common etymology, should not be conflated with the statistical concept of deviation.[20] Whereas the number of standard deviations from the mean is a strictly statistical matter, whether or not we consider an act (or, for that matter, a person) "deviant" is a pronouncedly moral (and, as such, cultural) one.

In sharp contrast to its statistical counterpart, the cultural notion of normality adds a pronouncedly evaluative dimension to the way we conceptualize it.[21] After all, whereas the strictly statistical notion of abnormality is value-neutral, the cultural notion of deviance is unmistakably negative. While both "A" and "F" students deviate statistically from the norm, only the latter are considered academically "deviant."

Conflating the statistical and cultural notions of normality may therefore explain why so many people are "driven by the desire . . . to know that [they are] normal"[22] (to the point of even raising the specter of a "tyranny of the normal"),[23] as well as why "the form that information must take to convince [them] that they are normal is statistical."[24] Indeed, as Warner points out,

> what faith was to the martyrs . . . normalcy is to the contemporary American. . . . One reason why you won't find many eloquent quotations about the desire to be normal in Shakespeare, or the Bible, or other common sources of moral wisdom, is that people didn't sweat much over being normal until the spread of statistics in the nineteenth century. Now they are surrounded by numbers that tell them what normal is: census figures, market demographics, opinion polls, social science studies, psychological surveys, clinical tests, sales figures, trends . . . the common man, the man on the street, the "heartland of America," etcetera. Under the conditions of mass culture, they are constantly bombarded by images of statistical populations and their norms, continually invited to make an implicit comparison between themselves and [others].[25]

The fundamental difference between the strictly statistical and distinctly cultural notions of normality raises the question whether the very terms *normal* and *abnormal* even belong in a scholarly vocabulary.[26] Indeed, as we are reminded, for example, by Alfred Kinsey, at least some of the sexual acts we label abnormal "prove, upon statistical examination, to occur in as many as . . . 75 per cent of certain populations," and it is therefore "difficult to maintain that such types of behavior are abnormal because they are rare."[27] That is also true of the way we use the prefixes *over-* and *under-* in words such as *overweight* and *underachiever*, thereby tacitly attributing the cultural stigma of deviance to phenomena that, strictly statistically speaking, may nevertheless still be "within normal limits."

Whereas culturally "abnormal" phenomena are semiotically marked, "normal" ones tend to remain unmarked.[28] As such, they come to be taken for granted.

That explains the pronouncedly asymmetrical manner whereby unmarked social identities come to be considered the *standard* or touchstone against which marked ones are characterized in terms of the extent to which they deviate from them,[29] as when actual bodies are compared against "cultural expectations about how human beings should look and act."[30] A classic example of such glaringly asymmetrical semiotic construction of identities is the conventional view of same-sex marriage as "a marked parallel to the unmarked, generic concept of marriage with its implicit assumption of heterosexuality."[31] Ironically, so is the way culture "reverses the markedness relations of biology" whereby an embryo "develop[s] into a female unless additional genetic information is supplied,"[32] so that men come to be conventionally considered "simply 'normal' people, unremarkable and unremarked upon,"[33] whereas women, while "born unmarked," are nevertheless "everywhere in the chains of markedness."[34]

By the same token, in America, whiteness is conventionally considered "a cultural default setting, the automatic point of comparison for any kind of difference,"[35] thereby constituting the standard of normality against which other ethnoracial

identities come to be conceptualized.[36] Whites are thus conceived as "phantom figure[s] against whom differences become
visible,"[37] the glaring asymmetry between the term *nonwhites*
and its nominally equivalent yet rarely used counterparts
non-blacks and *non-Asians* thereby underscoring the cultural
normality of whiteness and abnormality of blackness and
Asianness.

Consider also, along these lines, the pronouncedly asymmetrical conventional view of whites' speech as the unmarked,
standard, "normal" form of American English yet nonwhites'
speech as "accented":

> Everyone has an accent, but when an employer refuses to
> hire a person "with an accent," they are referring to a hidden
> norm of *non-accent*—a linguistic impossibility, but a socially
> constructed reality. People in power are perceived as speak-
> ing *normal, unaccented* English. Any speech that is different
> from that constructed norm is called an accent.[38]

The contrast between "standard" ("good," "correct") and "nonstandard" (such as Black or Puerto-Rican) English[39] exemplifies the unmistakably asymmetrical manner in which nonwhite
Americans are conventionally marked as "having an accent"
whereas white ones are considered unmarked, "normal" Americans who therefore have "no accent" at all.

To be unmarked thus means to be "the self-evident standard
against which all differences are measured,"[40] the "baselin[e]
against which to compare purportedly 'deviant' others"[41] in
terms of their distance from it. As evidenced even morpholog-
ically, unmarked terms (*father, host, true*) tend to be less conceptually complex than their marked counterparts (*stepfather,
hostess, untrue*),[42] and cognitively processing them therefore
requires less mental effort (as manifested in shorter processing

time),[43] since they actually constitute the foundational figurative baseline from which the latter are evidently derived.[44]

Marking, indeed, is "the way language alters the 'base meaning' of a word."[45] As perfect exemplars of "base words," unmarked terms (*man, male, he*) are therefore "fundamental and originative,"[46] whereas their marked counterparts (*woman, female, she*) are, after all, derived from them. The distinction between the unmarked and the marked thus captures the fundamental difference between the semiotically *basic* and the semiotically *derivative*.

Needless to say, *marked terms are typically introduced into the language only after their unmarked counterparts*, from which they are evidently derived. The term *documentary film*, for instance, could not have even been conceived earlier than its unmarked counterpart *film*, from which it was in fact derived. Nor could the introduction of the terms *watermelon, polar bear*, and *Memorial Day parade* have possibly preceded that of their unmarked counterparts *melon, bear*, and *parade*.

At the same time, however, note the glaring paucity of terms designed to denote phenomena we conventionally consider normal thereby tacitly assuming by default and taking for granted. Effectively regarded as literally un-remarkable, such phenomena are clearly not considered worth mentioning. Since they are essentially presumed, the terms that denote them therefore seem *culturally redundant* and thus *semiotically superfluous*.

That explains the inverse relation between normality and *nameability*. Whereas the normal needs no mentioning, the abnormal attracts considerable cultural attention and is thus specifically *labeled*. The term *Black English* (let alone *Ebonics*), for instance, has therefore no equivalent racialized counterpart such as *White English*, a term that, given the presumed normality of whiteness, would most likely be considered culturally redundant and thus semiotically superfluous.

Such glaring asymmetry also characterizes the semiotic relation between homo- and heterosexuality. Thus, whereas a Google search for the term *homoerotic*, for instance, yields 760,000 results, a parallel search for its nominally equivalent counterpart *heteroerotic* yields only 11,700.[47] And indeed, given our cultural default assumption of heteronormativity, it is clearly considered culturally redundant and therefore semiotically superfluous. By the same token, whereas searches for the terms *gay-friendly* and *gay marriage* yield 19,400,000 and 22,200,000 results, parallel searches for their nominally equivalent yet evidently culturally redundant counterparts *straight-friendly* and *straight marriage* yield only 65,400 and 89,500, respectively.[48]

Furthermore, only heteronormativity can explain the sharp contrast between the conventionally used term *same-sex marriage* and its nominally equivalent yet evidently culturally redundant and therefore semiotically superfluous counterpart *different-sex marriage*. Such striking disparity implies that the former term denotes an abnormal (and therefore literally re*mark*able) phenomenon in contrast to the "normal," culturally expected form of marriage denoted by the latter.[49]

The Shape of Normality

Although originally conceived in either/or, all-or-nothing terms, as so dramatically manifested in the strictly binary distinction between presence and absence of certain features, this way of thinking nevertheless represents only one possible way of theorizing markedness and unmarkedness. Both, after all, can also be conceptualized in terms of varying *degrees* of markedness, whereby a forty-sixth-birthday dinner party would be considered more marked than an ordinary dinner party yet less so than a fiftieth-birthday one. Furthermore, the marked can also represent the "extremes that stand out as either remarkably 'above' or remarkably 'below' the norm," whereas the unmarked can represent "the vast expanse of social reality" between them.[50]

Needless to say, the latter way of conceptualizing markedness and unmarkedness presupposes attributing structural equivalence to both the "positively" and "negatively" marked, thereby implying a fundamental asymmetry between the "edges" of a semiotic spectrum, which are considered special and therefore marked, and the rest of it, which is considered ordinary and therefore left unmarked. That is indeed why we have well-articulated cultural images of both excellence and deficiency yet no corresponding images of averageness. And while using labels such as *slut* and *virgin* to mark women who have "too much" or "exceptionally little" sex by conventional cultural standards, we have no cultural label to characterize those who are averagely-experienced:

> What do we call people who are at the other end of the spectrum from sluts? Prudes, perhaps. But "prude" too is a marked category. . . . There is no meaningful word for the middle of that . . . space that most people occupy most of the time. *Nameless* and characterless, the space we can loosely characterize as 'normal' is almost completely *undefined*.[51]

In a similar vein, we normally skew our moral attention[52] toward the "good" and the "bad" (thereby rewarding the former and punishing the latter) while remaining culturally indifferent toward what we consider morally neutral. We thus mark the exceptionally moral as well as the exceptionally immoral while leaving the amoral effectively unmarked. "'Saints' and 'sinners'" are thereby marked, whereas "the morally 'average' are not."[53] In short, "morally 'inferior' behavior, such as committing a crime, and morally 'superior' behavior, such as rescuing a person from a fire, are both marked; morally neutral behavior, such as walking on a city sidewalk, remains unmarked."[54]

Such profound semiotic asymmetry is even more elementary than the cognitive asymmetry between positivity and negativity,[55] which, after all, are *both* marked. As we are reminded by Durkheim, the distinction between the moral and the immoral pales in significance to the fundamental distinction between the sacred, which includes both of them, and the profane or amoral:

> In the history of human thought, there is no other example of two categories of things . . . as radically opposed to one another. The traditional opposition between good and evil is nothing beside this one: Good and evil are two opposed species of the same genus, namely morals. . . . [B]y contrast, the sacred and the profane are always and everywhere conceived . . . as separate genera, as two worlds with nothing in common.[56]

Any cultural asymmetry, in short, pales when compared to the one between the semiotically distinctive, or marked, and the semiotically neutral, or unmarked.

Such an effectively ternary model of marking, whereby both the "hyper-" and "hypo-" values of a semiotic object are marked, is fundamentally different from the binary model so perfectly embodied by the image of a tilted scale I have tacitly been using here in an effort to capture the notion of asymmetrically distributed semiotic "weight" (see figure 4.1). As such, it calls for an altogether different image to best capture its essentially threefold character.

Figure 4.1. The Asymmetrical Distribution of Semiotic "Weight"

It might be helpful, therefore, to consider the historical context in which the very notion of normality was in fact introduced. And indeed, as one might expect given our earlier discussion of markedness and atypicality, it is actually a product of the nineteenth-century advent of statistical thinking, and in particular of Carl Friedrich Gauss's vision of the so-called *normal distribution* so famously captured in the image of the bell-shaped "normal curve" along which we conventionally envision the way reality tends to be statistically distributed (see figure 4.2).[57] Indeed, as epitomized in Adolphe Quetelet's concept of "the average man,"[58] normality implies the fundamental contrast between averageness and "outlierness" so perfectly captured by this image.

Such an effectively ternary model of marking also reminds us that despite the fact that we valorize courage yet stigmatize cowardice, they are nevertheless semiotically parallel in that both of them are culturally marked. Although the moral

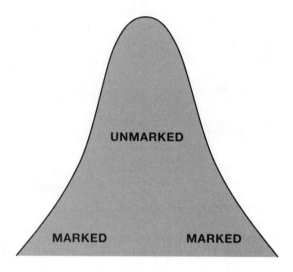

Figure 4.2. The "Normal" Distribution of Cultural Significance

qualities conventionally associated with each of them are pronouncedly antithetical, both of them nevertheless "stand out" in our minds.

Such an effectively ternary way of envisioning reality also helps us theorize the middle-aged, who are neither young nor old; emotional indifference, which involves neither love nor hate; and the middle class, who are neither rich nor poor. It likewise helps us envision intersubjectivity, which is neither subjective nor objective, let alone a cognitive sociology that avoids both the personal and universal aspects of the way we think.[59]

Normalizing and Othering

As so compellingly exemplified by the cross-cultural as well as intracultural variability in what is conventionally assumed by default and thereby taken for granted, *nothing is inherently normal* (or, for that matter, abnormal). Rather than being an inherent quality of maleness, whiteness, straightness, or able-bodiedness, for example, normality is socially attributed to them as part of a politico-semiotic process fittingly identified by Michel Foucault as *normalization*.[60]

Normalizing the unmarked involves *naturalizing*[61] (and thereby effectively essentializing) it by highlighting the supposedly universal as well as timeless nature of conventional standards of normality.[62] In fact, it is on the basis of its being presented to us as natural that we come to presume the unmarked and thereby take it for granted as "normal."

Yet the act of normalizing the unmarked is usually also accompanied by a parallel sociocognitive act of *abnormalizing* or *pathologizing* the marked. The process of establishing normality, in other words, is semiotically complemented by a process of abnormalizing "deviational 'special case[s]'" effectively characterized as something other than the unmarked.[63]

By marking something, we thus imply that it cannot be assumed by default and taken for granted, and as such is essentially "abnormal." And by so doing we thereby tacitly attribute normality to what remains unmarked.

In fact, ever since Georg Wilhelm Friedrich Hegel,[64] we have been theorizing the self in relation to "the other," and its identity as involving the attribution of alterity, or *otherness*, to various "others," as so perfectly exemplified in the case of gender.[65] By the same token, the notion of being "straight," for example, would have been utterly meaningless without its twin notion of "gay." Indeed, we cannot "conceptualize or define normality without reference to something from which 'normal' deviates."[66]

That explains the sociocognitive process aptly dubbed by Gayatri Spivak *othering*,[67] as exemplified by the use of the notion "animal" to help define "human." It likewise underscores the *semiotic exclusion* of the supposedly deviant, as when groups establish scapegoats[68] or conjure up monsters, those "spectacle[s] of abnormality" that seem to help delineate "the fault-lines of [their] identity."[69]

A classic case in point is the pathologization of the "corporeal other,"[70] conventionally *stigmatized* as deviant[71] (as so dramatically displayed in "freak shows"),[72] as part of the semiotic construction of "normal" bodies. A "narrative of universality surrounding bodies that correspond to notions of the ordinary" is thereby complemented by a "narrative of *deviance surrounding bodies considered different.*"[73] And like homosexual psyches undergoing "reparative therapy,"[74] culturally abnormal bodies are indeed often surgically "corrected":

> What is imagined as excess body fat, the effects of aging, marks of ethnicity such as supposedly Jewish noses, bodily particularities thought of as blemishes or deformities, and marks of history such as scarring and impairments are now expected to be surgically erased to *produce an unmarked body*.... This flight from the nonconforming body translates into individual *efforts to look normal, neutral, unmarked*, to not look disabled, queer, ugly, fat, ethnic, or raced.[75]

Ironically, we thus often consider surgically altered bodies "normal," and unmodified ones "abnormal."[76]

Language plays a major role in the process of othering:

> The terms Chinese American, Fundamentalist Protestant, Reagan Democrat, and Welfare Mother all imply . . . that the person is not really the . . . "typical" form of American, or Protestant, or Democrat, or mother. By making a compound form for a special type we also passively construct the normative case . . . by its *absence* of any linguistic qualifiers.[77]

Furthermore, the term *Chinese American* is more than just a lexical manifestation of an already-existing extrasemiotic, supposedly "real" asymmetry between Chinese Americanness and unmarked, "normal" Americanness. In fact, it helps establish such an essentialized sense of asymmetry in the first place!

To further appreciate the important role of language in the process of othering, consider also the unmistakably exclusionary term *non-Western*. Whereas a Google search for this term yields 3,020,000 results, a parallel search for its nominally equivalent counterpart *non-Eastern* yields only 19,900,[78] thereby tacitly exemplifying the conventional Western taken-for-grantedness of Westernness. Like the phrase *the West and the rest*, the very term *non-Western* implies the presumed normality (and therefore also cultural dominance) of everything Western[79] and corresponding abnormality of everything non-Western. As such, it is certainly one of the distinctive products of the pronouncedly Western-centric "Orientalist"[80] politico-semiotic project of effectively *exoticizing* "the Oriental other."

The symbiotic relationship between the twin processes of normalizing and othering is further exemplified by the way pathologizing same-sex desire helps normalize straightness. Given the fact that gays and lesbians are conventionally considered culturally abnormal "sexual others," it comes as no surprise that we have come to view heterosexuality as "the unremarkable outcome of a 'natural' process of growing up to feel desire for the opposite sex."[81]

As a result, the very same behavior that is considered unremarkable when performed by straights is often regarded as "flaunting" one's sexuality when performed by gays or lesbians.[82] And while a search for the term *flamboyant homosexuality* yields 7,220 results, a parallel search for its nominally equivalent yet culturally odd-sounding counterpart *flamboyant heterosexuality* yields only 89.[83] Indeed, as Bruni points out, "[a] straight woman puts a photograph of herself and her beloved on her desk at work and it's merely décor. A lesbian displays the same kind of picture and it's an act of laudable candor or questionable boldness: a statement, either way you cut it."[84] "I have every right to walk the streets of my neighborhood," he adds, "no matter whose fingers are interlaced with my own. Our clutch isn't a taunt or provocation. It's just an expression of tenderness—of basic humanity. In a world altered and advanced enough, it would be an innocuous, unnoticed part of the scenery."[85] In other words, it would be considered part of "the background"[86] and, as such, culturally unmarked.

The tremendous semiotic significance of the generalized "barbarian" for the ancient Greeks, the *gadjo* for Romanis, the *odar* for Armenians, and the *goy* (gentile) for Jews likewise exemplifies the inseparability of ethnic (or, for that matter, ethnonational) normality and abnormality. A perfect case in point is the cultural construction of unmarked, "normal" Americanness along with a parallel, contrasting notion of marked, "abnormal" Americanness implicit in the following tacitly anti-elite, populist remark made by the 2008 Republican vice-presidential nominee Sarah Palin: "We believe that the best of America is in these small towns . . . and in these wonderful little pockets of what I call *the real America*."[87] Such "real" Americanness is often equated with nativeness, thereby effectively excluding immigrants and descendants of recent immigrants, as exemplified by the use of quotation marks as well as the subtly condescending adjective *new* to mark and thereby "otherize" such "abnormal" Americans in the following statement made during the 2014 World Cup by right-wing commentator Ann Coulter:

If more *"Americans"* are watching soccer today, it's only because of the demographic switch effected by Teddy Kennedy's 1965 immigration law. I promise you: No *American* whose great-grandfather was born here is watching soccer. One can only hope that, in addition to learning English, these *new Americans* will drop their soccer fetish with time.[88]

Yet as ironically evidenced by those literally labeled "Native Americans," while non-nativeness is clearly a most distinctive characteristic of such "abnormal" Americans, so is their nonwhiteness. After all, Coulter's soccer-watching, quotation-marked "new" Americans were most probably Latinos, while the implicitly white small-town and rural dwellers of those "wonderful little pockets" of Palin's "real America" tacitly provided a striking, spectacularly evocative contrast to the ethnoracially "abnormal" Democratic presidential candidate, whom she evidently considered at best nominally yet certainly not "really" American. (Indeed, soon after Obama assumed the presidency, the Tea Party slogan "I want my America back" was born.) Given the cultural dominance of leukonormativity, "real," "normal," unmarked Americans are presumably white.[89] While their whiteness may be "unspoken," it is nevertheless assumed.[90]

Indeed, members of different ethnoracial groups are actually inducted into "normal," unmarked Americanness quite differently depending on their group's envisioned proximity to or distance from whiteness. Had Donald Trump lived at the time of Martin Van Buren, Theodore Roosevelt, or Franklin Roosevelt, for example, he most probably would not have so adamantly insisted that they actually produce their birth certificates as he in fact demanded that Obama do, as their Dutch roots would clearly not have clashed with his presumed notion of "normal" Americanness the way Obama's African ones evidently did.

The fact that, unlike many other descendants of immigrants, neither Van Buren nor the Roosevelts evidently felt compelled to "Americanize" their noticeably Dutch last names further indicates that the social pressure to shed one's ethnicity in order to become fully assimilated into what Israel Zangwill so aptly dubbed the American "melting pot" is applied asymmetrically, as only nonwhite immigrants are actually expected to "melt" their own ethnoracial identity[91] in order to become qualified to assume a "normal," unmarked one. Whereas Dutch (not to mention English) immigrants have been granted full-fledged Americanness almost immediately upon arrival, that has certainly not been true of those conventionally considered nonwhite—the Jews, Irish, and Italians until not that long ago,[92] or Africans, Asians,[93] and Latinos to this day. That also explains why many Americans know very well who was their country's first African American president yet have no idea who was the first Dutch American one.

Representativeness

Albert Einstein once quipped that "[i]f my theory of relativity is proven successful, Germany will claim me as a German and France will declare that I am a citizen of the world. Should my theory prove untrue, France will say that I am a German and Germany will declare that I am a Jew."[94]

Indeed, we tend to view people as somehow "*representative*" of others who share their marked identities. Members of culturally marked social categories are thus often seen as "representing" other members of those categories (which is why fat characters, for example, are played by fat actors),[95] whereas members of unmarked ones tend to be seen as representing "people in general," thereby reinforcing the illusion that women, African Americans, gays and lesbians, and people with disability, for instance, constitute various deviations from normality, whereas men, Euro-Americans, straights, and the able-bodied, by contrast, are simply ordinary, "normal" people.[96]

That certainly provides a window into the extra-logical, unmistakably sociosemiotic underpinnings of *generalizability*. It thus explains, for example, why findings of medical studies done on women are rarely generalized to conclusions about humans in general whereas those of studies done on men often are.[97] It also explains why during World War II the United States interned Japanese- but not German- or Italian-Americans, as well as why after Timothy McVeigh's bombing of the Murrah Federal Building in Oklahoma City no one demanded tighter security measures against Christian Americans.[98]

By the same token, as Peggy McIntosh has famously characterized the condition of being white in America, "I can swear, or dress in second hand clothes, or not answer letters, without having people attribute these choices to the bad morals, the poverty, or the illiteracy of my race."[99] For the same reason, we rarely view white serial killers as "reflecting the 'sociopathic tendency' of 'white culture,'"[100] or expect "moderate whites" to publicly condemn mass shooters the way "moderate Muslims" are often expected to publicly condemn Muslim terrorists, despite the fact that both serial killers and mass shooters tend to be white. Indeed, we often attribute mass shootings to mental illness, which we conventionally consider an individualized condition rather than one that characterizes an entire group.

Nonwhites, however, tend to be viewed as "representative" of other nonwhites,[101] and when a character's ethnoracial identity is not specified in a play or a script, white actors, for example, are far more likely than nonwhite ones to be cast in that role.[102] Indeed, when black actress Noma Dumezweni was cast in the role of Hermione Granger in a theatrical production of J. K. Rowling's *Harry Potter and the Cursed Child*, the author felt compelled to remind her fans that "white skin" was actually "never specified" in her book.[103]

As so plainly exemplified by Halloween costumes and ethnic jokes, perhaps most revealing in this regard is the pronouncedly asymmetrical abundance of stereotypes of marked identities compared to those of unmarked ones. We thus have very distinct cultural stereotypes of Asians, lesbians, and drug addicts, for example, yet rarely ones of straights, law-abiding citizens, the mentally healthy, or the able-bodied—a glaring asymmetry that underscores the relative semiotic ease at which we evidently construct stereotypes of cultural abnormality compared to those of cultural normality.

Neutrality and Invisibility

Since first theorized by Trubetzkoy and Jakobson, unmarkedness has been associated with the absence of identifiable characteristics ("distinctive features") and, thus, with its generic, effectively *neutral* character. As exemplified by the semiotic battles over "Merry *Christmas*" and "Happy *Holidays*" or "*Black* Lives Matter" and "*All* Lives Matter," whereas markedness implies specificity, normalizing the unmarked (and, as we shall see, solidifying its cultural dominance) involves genericizing or "neutralizing" it.[104]

A perfect example is the conventional view of maleness as a supposedly gender-neutral "standard or norm for . . . the species as a whole," and femaleness as but a "deviation from that . . . standard."[105] Thus, whereas the words *woman* or *she*, for instance, denote only females, their masculine equivalents (*man, he*) are also used to denote humans in general, as in *Man has the capacity to reason*, or in *When someone is sick he needs a lot of rest*.[106]

As exemplified by generic drugs, genericity is often manifested in *namelessness*. Conventionally regarded as a standard of normality, the unmarked therefore often remains nameless, as only that which deviates from the standard is considered remark-able enough to actually be labeled. In sharp contrast to the term *women's literature*, for instance, the term *men's literature* thus sounds semiotically superfluous, and whereas a Google search for the former yields 425,000 results, a parallel search for the latter indeed yields only 21,600.[107] By the same token, whereas searches for the terms *women candidates* and *women's history* yield 522,000 and 17,600,000 results, parallel searches for their nominally equivalent yet culturally redundant counterparts *men candidates* and *men's history* yield only 27,100 and 76,400, respectively.[108]

Consider also, along these lines, the conventional genericization of heterosexuality, as so spectacularly exemplified by the glaring asymmetry between the emergence of the field of "gay and lesbian studies" and the utter absence of a nominally equivalent yet nonetheless culturally redundant field of "straight studies,"[109] or the fact that, in sharp contrast to the term *gay and lesbian literature*, the term *straight literature* seems semiotically superfluous. Indeed, we rarely even consider heterosexuality a sexual "orientation," a notion we tend to associate with sexual preferences that deviate from the supposedly generic ones conventionally deemed "normal."

By the same token, consider also the genericization of whiteness (such as in America),[110] so that whereas being black or Asian, for example, is conventionally racialized, being white is considered racially "neutral."[111] After all, as one is reminded by the common etymology of the French and Spanish words for "white" (*blanc, blanco*) and the word *blank*, white is not even considered a color,[112] and "[t]he idea of whiteness as neutrality [therefore] suggests its usefulness for designating a social group that is to be taken for the human ordinary."[113] Indeed, like other unmarked identities, whiteness is often defined in terms of absence,[114] with whites being considered essentially colorless, as so perfectly exemplified by the very term *people of color*:

> Consider the phrase "people of color." . . . [W]hat is its unmarked equivalent? . . . [T]here is no such thing as a colorless person. *"People who are not of color" are the baseline, the default, the unexceptional, the normal.* The unmarked category against which "people of color" are tacitly opposed are "notcolored" people; in other words, whites.[115]

As a result, in America, one's race is somehow considered far more salient when one is black or Asian, for example, than when one is white, just as one's gender or sexual orientation is considered far more salient when one is female or gay than when one is male or straight. And just as we tend to associate gender primarily with women, thereby conventionally considering them somehow more "gendered" than men, we also tend to view race as something that "people of color have" yet "white people lack."[116] Indeed, *"[t]o be white in America is not to have to think about it. . . .* [T]he meaning of being white is having the choice of attending to or ignoring one's own whiteness."[117]

Conventionally equated with being white, being simply "American" thus implies being ethnoracially "neutral." Hence the notion of the "generic American"[118] implicit in the pronouncedly asymmetrical conventional distinction between "hyphenated" (that is, marked) and "unhyphenated"[119] (that is, unmarked), supposedly ethnoracially neutral forms of Americanness, as when people of English or German, yet rarely West African or Filipino, descent are considered simply "Americans." As an Asian American teenager explains, "*An American is white.* [When] people say, hey, so-and-so is dating an 'American,' [y]ou know she's dating a white boy."[120] By the same token, in sharp contrast to Jewish American or Indian American weddings, for instance, Anglo-American ones are conventionally associated with the so-called "*general* customs" of American society,[121] thereby effectively being perceived as "ordinary," supposedly generic, ethnically neutral "American" weddings.

Such notion of generic, ethnically "neutral" Americanness is implied, of course, in the very idea of cultural *assimilation*, a process specifically characterized by Ashley Doane as "the shedding of ethnicity amid absorption into the ethnically neutral 'larger society.'"[122] In undergoing such a process, immigrants indeed try to shed their ethnic identities (as manifested in their pronouncedly marked names, food, garb, and traditional customs), thereby displaying their readiness to assume an unmarked, "de-ethnicized" one. The fact that traditionally Italian foods such as spaghetti and macaroni, for instance, are not relegated to "ethnic" sections of American supermarkets (unlike, say, gefilte fish or tikka masala sauce) is thus indicative of the extent to which they have in fact been assimilated into the unmarked, generic, supposedly ethnically neutral "American" cuisine.

Since they "serve as the standard by which others [are] marked by their difference," people whose identities are culturally unmarked "often experience the sense that they lack an identity"[123] (for the same reason that only cultures that are "different from [the] norm" are actually "marked as 'cultures'").[124] Given their supposed "neutrality," many whites are therefore less likely than blacks, Asians, or Latinos, for example, to identify themselves as members of a distinct ethnoracial category. As a result, they do not even view themselves as having a distinct ethnoracial identity.[125]

In fact, *unmarked identities are not even considered identities* (which explains the lack of a special term for people who, in sharp contrast to the distinctly marked "homeless," *do* have a home, regardless of whether or not they own it). Rarely, for example, would we ever characterize someone as "able-bodied" or "averagely experienced."[126] And as exemplified by the fact that a Google search for the term *the LGBT community* yields 4,360,000 results whereas a parallel one for its nominally equivalent yet culturally redundant counterpart *the straight community* yields only 38,900,[127] nor does straightness constitute a distinct cultural identity.[128]

As but a manifestation of cultural inattention, unmarkedness implies a certain degree of cultural *invisibility*.[129] And indeed, as ironically captured by the metaphor of a whiteout, which makes it "difficult to see anything except very dark objects,"[130] unmarked features such as whiteness are often culturally invisible.[131]

Yet while whites' ethnoracial membership may in fact be inattended to by (and thereby effectively invisible to) group members themselves,[132] nonwhites are actually quite aware of it.[133] Thus, while Israel's culturally and politically dominant Ashkenazim, for example, may indeed not consider themselves a distinctly identifiable group, their ethnicity is by no means invisible to the "Mizrahim, Ethiopians, Palestinians, and . . . all the 'others' who do not benefit from the same advantages as Ashkenazim do."[134] After all,

> *in an ethnicized social system, all actors are ethnicized, including the ones who do not perceive themselves as such.* The lack of ethnic consciousness does not indicate that ethnicity is not a relevant category in their lives. Rather, the . . . "nonethnic" self-definition suggests that many Ashkenazim regard themselves as the benchmark of Israeliness, representing the nation in its entirety. By denying their ethnocultural visibility, [they] conflate Ashkenaziness with the national collective.[135]

This brings us back to the relation between unmarkedness and social dominance. As exemplified by the way in which the absence of a distinctive country code marking American web addresses tacitly reflects America's Internet dominance, one of the major privileges enjoyed by dominant groups is that of remaining nameless[136] and, more generally, culturally invisible,[137] which therefore helps them evade scrutiny. Being essentially taken for granted, their privileged status is thereby effectively kept from being questioned, let alone explicitly challenged, since it is hard to question what is hidden from view.[138] Their very dominance, in other words, thus partly depends on their cultural invisibility.[139]

Social dominance, in short, involves the privilege of being considered "normal" and thereby assumed by default and taken for granted. As such, it entails the ability to protect a group's assumed normality from being challenged.

Being culturally invisible (such as by effectively inhabiting unmarked, supposedly generic and therefore "neutral" bodies) is thus critical to the way maleness, for example, both establishes and maintains its social dominance.[140] It is likewise critical to the by-and-large similar dominance of straightness.

Straights, after all, "have the unparalleled privilege of being able to go about [their] lives without [their] relationship attracting notice,"[141] and such cultural invisibility therefore makes "heterosexual pairing . . . difficult to reflect on objectively as simply one of many possible ways of organising social life."[142] To be straight, in other words, is to have the option of effectively disregarding one's straightness:

> One main way privilege works is for heterosexuals to view their identities as neither identities nor forms of privilege. Since heterosexuals are able to take for granted their unacknowledged privilege, heterosexual rituals, social norms, and other behaviors go *unseen* as mechanisms through which heterosexual identity is made dominant in daily and institutional life.[143]

Such cultural invisibility is also critical to the way whiteness both establishes and maintains its social dominance[144] by having white people essentially portrayed "as 'individuals,' not members of a privileged racial group marked with the social status and prestige of normality."[145] As a result, we come to view race and other forms of ethnicity as almost exclusive attributes of "minorities," thereby effectively marking nonwhites as "ethnic"[146] or "raced" while considering whites ethnoracially "neutral," with race supposedly playing no role in their lives.[147]

Self-Evidence and Cognitive Hegemony

By both establishing and maintaining such effectively hegemonic sense of normality,[148] social dominance thus helps achieve *cognitive hegemony*,[149] so spectacularly characterized by *the power to otherize* anything that deviates from a certain standard of normality as well as *the power to affect what others take for granted* by essentially leading them to almost habitually make certain tacit assumptions without even realizing that they are making them.[150] And the fact that such ultimately conventional sense of normality is nevertheless culturally assumed by default and thereby taken for granted is indeed what makes such hegemony so striking.

Default assumptions are formidable mechanisms of establishing as well as maintaining cognitive hegemony, as it is much harder to question, let alone challenge, the *implicit*.[151] As exemplified by terms or phrases such as *naturally, surely, obviously, of course*, or *needless to say*, taken-for-grantedness projects a sense of *self-evidence*.[152] Based on some implied prior agreement supposedly shared with everyone else, it is effectively "exempt from the need for supporting evidence" and thereby relatively shielded from challenge.[153]

And indeed, despite its merely conventional nature, hegemonic normality (what we consider "*common sense*")[154] is nevertheless presented in *absolute* terms,[155] which makes it seem indisputable, as "[r]ival views become unimaginable."[156] The term *alternative medicine*, for example, thus presumes the absolute validity of Western medicine (which we in fact conventionally refer to as simply *medicine*), whereas the terms *alternative newspaper* and *alternative music*, let alone *alternative lifestyle* and *alternative family structure*, tacitly presume the absolute normality of their unmarked, "mainstream" counterparts.

By marking some regions of our phenomenal world while leaving the others unmarked, cognitive hegemony thus involves the power to both abnormalize and normalize. As we shall now see, however, it is in fact possible to also resist it, ironically enough, by abnormalizing what we conventionally consider normal as well as normalizing what we conventionally consider abnormal.

5

Semiotic Subversion

To whom have you disclosed your heterosexual tendencies? How did they react?

—Martin Rochlin, "Heterosexual Questionnaire"

Despite their hegemonic grip on our minds, however, conventional marking patterns are sometimes also challenged, as exemplified by various efforts to deliberately *subvert conventional semiotic asymmetries*. Such subversion involves the use of one of two major semiotic tactics specifically designed to alter the relative "weights" of the upper and lower pans of the proverbial scale featured in figure 4.1 vis-à-vis each other.

Marking the Unmarked

The more common such tactic involves *marking the hitherto unmarked*[1] thereby making it semiotically "weighty" (see figure 5.1), as exemplified by Ivanka Trump's attempt to recast her father as an equal-opportunity rather than a specifically misogynous insulter: "People ask me . . . 'He said this and this about women,' and I've said, 'Have you looked at the things he's said about men?'"[2] Doing that entails turning the proverbial spotlight on what we habitually ignore thereby making it an object of our explicit awareness. Such a *gestalt switch*[3] makes things seem to "jum[p] *out of the background* enough to be perceived consciously rather than just being part of [our] surroundings."[4] Effectively reversing our habitual way of experiencing

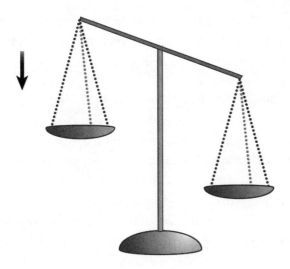

Figure 5.1. Semiotic Subversion I: Marking the Hitherto Unmarked

the background-like regions of our phenomenal world, it thus involves *foregrounding*.[5]

As exemplified by the ratio of the gendered parts of our body to the gender-neutral ones,[6] or holidays to ordinary days, what we mark and therefore explicitly notice is proportionally smaller than what is left unmarked and thereby implicitly ignored.[7] The marked regions of our phenomenal world thus receive glaringly disproportionate amounts of cultural attention relative to their size, while the typically larger unmarked ones hardly receive any notice.[8] Marking, in other words, "strangles [our] awareness [by] limit[ing] us to seeing only a fraction of what there is to be seen."[9] Like fisheye lenses that help broaden our peripheral vision,[10] foregrounding, by contrast, expands what we notice.

As the semiotic equivalent of the background-like, habitually inattended to components of our phenomenal world[11] (our ordinary surroundings, the constant sound of our breathing), the unmarked is unremarkable and, as such, effectively unnoticeable. Nevertheless, it is not inherently so, and can in fact become quite noticeable.

That, however, requires a deliberate effort to actually *notice what we habitually take for granted* by *refraining from presuming what we normally do*. Given the implicit nature of what we assume by default and thereby take for granted, that presupposes an effort to *make the implicit explicit*. In other words, it requires paying conscious attention to, being explicitly aware of.[12]

This calls for "educat[ing] the senses to *see the ordinary as extraordinary [and] the familiar as strange*," as the early Romantic poet Friedrich von Hardenberg, or Novalis, so aptly put it,[13] since only when the familiar is estranged can we actively notice it. Such fundamental *assumption reversal* presupposes the cognitive process referred to by Viktor Shklovsky as *defamiliarization* or *estrangement*.[14] As a conscious effort to achieve "a new look at the same old world," it involves "invert[ing] . . . the everyday ways of looking [that] render the world a . . . familiar place."[15]

That, of course, calls for a more deliberative mode of thinking[16] than our habitual and therefore fundamentally automatic one.[17] In other words, it presupposes a process of cognitive *deautomatization*,[18] which entails *refraining from taking our default assumptions for granted*[19]—a process effectively analogous to the one comically featured in Gary Larson's "Far Side" cartoon *Basic Lives*, which foregrounds via thought balloons the tacit thoughts[20] of a man walking ("Left foot, right foot, left foot, right foot"), a frog hopping ("Hop, rest, hop, rest"), a bird flapping its wings while flying ("Up, down, up, down, up, down"), and a dog barking ("Bark, don't bark, bark, don't bark"),[21] thereby reminding us that what we have come to regard as inherently and therefore inevitably unmarked is anything but.

The Politics of Foregrounding

Foregrounding plays a major role in the epistemically subversive process of consciousness- or *awareness-raising*.[22] While the 32,800 results yielded by my previously mentioned Google search for the culturally redundant and therefore semiotically superfluous term *openly straight* are indeed considerably fewer than the 3,740,000 results for its nominally equivalent counterpart *openly gay*, the very fact that such a term is nevertheless featured on 32,800 websites is actually quite remarkable. The lexical marking of such a traditionally unmarked notion as "open straightness" is an unmistakably political statement specifically designed to challenge its presumed cultural redundancy.

Consider also, along these lines, the deliberate attempt to semiotically subvert leukonormativity by marking the traditionally unmarked notion of whiteness, as when using the term *historically white colleges*[23] to foreground (and thereby tacitly challenge the presumed normality of) the culturally redundant and therefore semiotically superfluous equivalent of the common term *historically black colleges*, or for that matter when Morgan Freeman, having been asked about Black History Month, wryly shot back, "Which month is *White* History Month?"[24] His sarcastic allusion to this nonexistent month was an attempt to subversively foreground the glaringly asymmetrical tacit portrayal of black American history as distinct and therefore separate from "American" history yet white American history as essentially synonymous with it, thereby deeming the very notion of a "White History Month" culturally redundant and the term itself semiotically superfluous. Such asymmetry, of course, tacitly also deems African Americans distinct from "ordinary," unmarked ones thereby effectively othering them. By defying the very distinction between

American and *black* American history, Freeman therefore challenged the tacit exclusion of African Americans from the category "American." By mockingly alluding to a "White History Month" he thus helped lay bare the presumed normality of whiteness in America.

Foregrounding whiteness also helps lay bare the glaring asymmetry whereby black criminals are conventionally reduced to their blackness whereas white ones are afforded "the privilege of individualization."[25] As Tim Wise pointed out after the Columbine massacre, the fact that the school shooters were all white

> has gone without mention. . . . [W]e hear [that] all the shooters were boys; all the shooters used guns; all the shooters talked openly about violence; all the shooters played violent video games [yet] the racial similarities between [them] was irrelevant. While we can rest assured these kids would have been "raced" had they come from black "ghetto matriarchs" . . . it seems as though no one can see the most obvious common characteristic among them: namely, their white skin.[26]

Such glaring asymmetry has likewise led political commentator Chris Hayes to mockingly blame "the white community" for not being more outspoken against violent crimes committed by whites.[27]

Consider also, along these lines, the explicit cultural emergence in the 1970s and 1980s of the proverbial "straight white male." Sally Robinson describes the relatively recent fall of straight white maleness from its traditional position as the embodiment of heteronormative, leukonormative, and andronormative visions of normality (that is, as "a disembodied universality," the unmarked, supposedly neutral standard against which all other identities were otherized) to its current one as but "an embodied specificity":[28]

> Whereas white male novelists . . . might have until recently been read simply as "novelists," many might now find themselves categorically defined *as* white male novelists: they might find themselves *marked*, not read for their expression of a personal, individualized vision but, like women writers or African American writers, habitually read as the exemplars of a particularized—gendered and racialized—perspective.[29]

A somewhat similar semiotic calculus in fact also led televangelist Jerry Falwell to deliberately name and thereby foreground the hitherto unmarked and therefore culturally invisible conservative social movement he helped launch in 1979 "The Moral Majority."[30] It likewise led the 2011 Occupy movement to use the term *The 99 Percent* to explicitly foreground the hitherto unmarked millions of Americans effectively excluded from the culturally marked income category "The Top 1 Percent."[31]

Language clearly plays a pivotal role in the process of foregrounding. As exemplified, for instance, by the way Whole Foods stores mark their nonorganic food products with the sign "Conventional," foregrounding the hitherto unmarked often involves simply *naming* it.[32]

Consider also, along these lines, the tremendous cultural and political significance of the actual introduction of the term *sexual harassment*. As we are reminded by Catharine MacKinnon, "Until 1976, lacking a term to express it, sexual harassment was literally unspeakable, which made a generalized, shared, and social definition of it, inaccessible."[33] It was the very act of *labeling* it, therefore, that actually gave this hitherto unmarked and therefore still preconceptualized phenomenon a cultural life.

As a semiotic "eye-opener,"[34] naming, in short, helps make the hitherto unmarked culturally "visible."[35] Given the fact that while unplanned pregnancies have traditionally been referred to as "accidents" there is still no equivalent term for planned ones, for instance, the tremendous politico-semiotic significance of the very name "Planned Parenthood," indeed, is quite obvious. By the same token, the terms *carnism*[36] (or *vegaphobia*[37]) and *speciesism*[38] are specifically designed to foreground (and thereby challenge the presumed normality of) the traditionally unmarked cultural opposites of vegetarianism and animal-rights activism.

As further evidenced by the use of the term *heterosexual* or *straight* to semiotically mark and thereby effectively abnormalize a sexual orientation conventionally considered normal, naming also helps *de-naturalize* it.[39] Using this term essentially defies the givenness and therefore axiomatic presumption of straightness.[40] As such, it challenges the very "rhetorical opposition of what is ... 'natural' and what is 'derivative' or 'contrived'" by demonstrating that heterosexuality "must itself be treated as a dependent term."[41]

The same is also true of the use of the term *able-bodied* to tacitly challenge able-bodied normativity. Like characterizing anyone who is not autistic as "neurotypical," using this term treats "ordinary" individuals as objects of explicit cultural attention thereby tacitly putting them on an *equal semiotic footing* with disabled ones. This is even more pronounced in the case of terms such as *non-blind*[42] or *non-wheelies*,[43] let alone *non-disabled*,[44] which, like *not homosexual*,[45] effectively transform conventionally unmarked "normal" individuals into an explicitly marked and therefore semiotically abnormalized category, thereby tacitly challenging their conventionally nonderivative (that is, "basic"), taken-for-granted epistemic status.

Indeed, not only are conventionally unmarked "normals" marked as "able-bodied" or simply "abled," but they are sometimes also labeled *temporarily abled*,[46] a term specifically designed to blur the very distinction between "able-bodied" and "disabled." As "a stark reminder that each of us stands vulnerable to the physical diminishments provoked by disease, accident, or simply the inevitable processes of aging,"[47] it tacitly defies the supposedly binary distinction between our conventional notions of able-bodiedness and disability.[48] After all,

> [t]he fact is that most citizens will have some level of impairment. . . . Most humans, as they age, will find themselves less able to see, hear, walk, or think so well as they did before. One disability activist recently spoke at a convention to "normal" people and said, ". . . Come back in twenty years and a lot of you will be with us!"[49]

Marking the hitherto unmarked often involves *adding an adjective* thereby effectively "abnormalizing" what is habitually assumed by default and therefore taken for granted. Consider, for example, in this regard the semiotically subversive use of the term *vanilla sex*[50] to denote "ordinary" sexual practices. By explicitly marking them, using this term thus defies their conventionally presumed normality. In other words, by the very act of naming practices conventionally deemed "normal," it challenges their presumed genericity.

In so doing, of course, it tacitly also helps normalize what is conventionally considered "abnormal" behavior. By explicitly marking "normal" and therefore conventionally unmarked sexual practices, using the term *vanilla sex* effectively puts them on an equal semiotic footing with their conventionally marked less "bland" counterparts thereby implicitly making the latter more culturally acceptable.[51]

Marking the conventionally unmarked, in short, helps normalize the conventionally marked, as further exemplified by the use of the term *cisgender* to refer to people whose gender identity conforms with their birth-assigned sex.[52] Like both *neurotypical* and *straight*, the term helps "de-centralize the dominant group, exposing it as merely one possible alternative rather than the 'norm' against which trans people are defined."[53] In other words, it casts transgender and "cisgender" persons as categorical equals.[54] Assigning the latter a distinct label and thereby effectively putting conventionally marked "trans" identities and conventionally unmarked "ordinary" ones on an equal semiotic footing tacitly helps normalize the former by subverting the latter's presumed normality and therefore cultural privilege of remaining unnamed.

Academic Foregrounding

The effort to "abnormalize" and thereby foreground what we conventionally take for granted is often pursued academically,[55] reminding us that, as Marcel Proust famously observed, "[t]he only true voyage of discovery" may very well be "not to visit strange lands but to possess other eyes"[56] and thereby "find surprises lurking [even] in ostensibly obvious observations."[57] It has thus led anthropologist Edward Hall, for example, to explicitly focus his academic gaze on the essentially implicit and therefore hitherto unexplored social organization of interpersonal distance.[58] It has likewise inspired Erving Goffman's virtually unprecedented explorations of the conventionally taken-for-granted social rules and rituals underlying face-to-face interaction,[59] which, in drawing scholarly attention to "ordinary persons doing ordinary things,"[60] effectively pioneered a sociology of "everyday life" whose expressed goal is *to make the familiar strange*:

> [T]he ordinary, mundane and "everyday" social world—the familiar—is made "strange" in order that it can be systematically analysed and explored. Hence *taken-for-granted assumptions . . . are subjected to a sociological gaze . . .* whereby "normal" and "expected" ways of doing things are problematized or questioned, and where familiar understandings of social life are challenged.[61]

That, of course, calls for explicit explorations of implicit, habitual, background-like occurrences and activities that are "so mundane, so taken-for-granted, so normal, that most people, including scholars, fail to appreciate their significance."[62] And as I keep telling my students, it also calls for doing our best to suspend our default, habitual outlook on the world and assume the epistemic standpoint of the proverbial Martian in order to become more explicitly aware of the numerous taken-for-granted assumptions we tacitly make.

Consider, next, the deliberate efforts by feminists "to *question what passes as ordinary . . .* in order to unsettle the ground upon which norms hold sway"[63] and thereby challenge the unmarkedness and therefore taken-for-grantedness of maleness,[64] which led in the 1980s to the emergence of the field of men's or masculinities studies as part of a vigorous academic assault on andronormativity. Men, of course, had been studied long before that, yet as generic humans rather than specifically *as men*.[65] By making maleness explicit rather than merely implicit,[66] feminism has thus tacitly challenged its presumed normality.

The emergence of men's studies has likewise inspired the somewhat analogous emergence of whiteness studies,[67] yet another relatively recent academic field of inquiry that, quite similarly, tacitly challenges the presumed normality and therefore also both the unmarkedness and taken-for-grantedness of being white. Like men, whites had also been studied long before the 1980s, yet as generic humans rather than specifically *as whites*.[68] As Ruth Frankenberg, one of the first students of whiteness, would later reflect on the epistemic significance of foregrounding it,

> My research engages whiteness [but] the statement "my research engages whiteness" could not have been made, meaningfully, at the time, around 1980, when I began [my] inquiry. . . . This is so because, at that moment, the notion of "whiteness" was not present in the political or intellectual worlds of which I was a part.[69]

Consider also in this regard Rosina Lippi-Green's critique of "the myth of non-accent."[70] After all, she insists, *"every native speaker of US English has an accent,* no matter how unmarked the person's language may *seem* to be."[71] Though she herself is conventionally perceived as having no accent, she adds, in fact "I do have an accent. My English tells anybody [that] I am a white woman . . . who has lived most of her life . . . in the midwest."[72] And just as in the cases of using the terms *neurotypical, vanilla sex,* and *cisgender,* by specifically marking her conventionally unmarked and therefore supposedly generic ethnoracial identity she thus tacitly also helps normalize its conventionally marked "accented" counterparts.

Effectively completing the cultural emergence of the proverbial "straight white male," the 1980s also saw the beginning of the somewhat analogous academic assault on heteronormativity famously anticipated four decades earlier by Alfred Kinsey, who was evidently far more interested in understanding "why people did not become involved in *every* form of sexual behavior" than "why they preferred a partner of one sex rather than the other."[73] And the main motivation underlying such epistemically subversive fundamental assumption reversal, indeed, was to foreground and thereby "make visible . . . the mundane quotidian actions that result in the routine achievement of a taken-for-granted world that socially excludes or marginalizes non-heterosexuals."[74]

Like both men and whites, straights, of course, had also been studied well before the 1980s, yet not specifically *as straights*. Adrienne Rich's classic 1980 essay "Compulsory Heterosexuality and Lesbian Existence,"[75] for example, would have therefore been almost inconceivable at the time, as would books such as Chrys Ingraham's *Thinking Straight: The Power, the Promise, and the Paradox of Heterosexuality*,[76] Hanne Blank's *Straight: The Surprisingly Short History of Heterosexuality*,[77] James Dean's *Straights: Heterosexuality in Post-Closeted Culture*,[78] or Louis-Georges Tin's *The Invention of Heterosexual Culture*.[79] The deliberate effort to foreground the social construction of straightness as a taken-for-granted ordinary phenomenon[80] certainly underlies such attempts to culturally and historically contextualize heteronormativity's hegemonic grip on our minds. Jonathan Katz in fact describes his book *The Invention of Heterosexuality* as an attempt to introduce a distinctly "heterosexual history that [would be] *explored, rather than simply taken for granted*."[81] Sue Wilkinson and Celia Kitzinger's idea of actually inviting a number of straight authors to explicitly reflect on their traditionally untheorized identity as heterosexuals[82] was likewise part of a deliberate, epistemically subversive effort to abandon one of our culture's most fundamental default assumptions (heteronormativity) and effectively challenge the presumed normality and therefore taken-for-grantedness of heterosexuality.

Given the essentially asynchronous manner in which contrastive pairs of terms often come into being, it is particularly noteworthy that when Karl-Maria Kertbeny coined in 1868 the terms *homosexual* and *heterosexual*, he actually introduced them simultaneously, thereby effectively putting them on an equal semiotic footing. In fact, he did that on purpose, since, as we saw in the cases of both *neurotypical* and *cisgender*, "having two marked categories . . . generates a certain amount of equality, which was precisely his point"[83] as well as that of anybody who explicitly studies heterosexuality.

As products of the 1980s, the studies of maleness, whiteness, and straightness have been parts of the same deliberate academic effort to "turn a critical eye on unmarked categories . . . that assume a normative . . . character in everyday life"[84] and thereby challenge fundamental conventional assumptions such as andronormativity, leukonormativity, and heteronormativity. In fact, Harry Brod's teaching philosophy explicitly stresses the inherent relatedness of such assumptions:

> I want my students to understand that men are gendered too. . . . To let the study of gender be equivalent to the study of women is to leave men as unmarked by gender and hence normatively human. . . . Once [students] have internalized this model, a study of race, for example, can no longer be mistaken solely for a study of people of color. Students will now come to see whites as being raced as well. Further . . . they come to see that the commonly posed question "What causes homosexuality?" . . . takes as norm and leaves uninterrogated the dominant category of heterosexuality.[85]

This striking semiotic parallel between the default assumptions we sometimes make about race and gender, indeed, is also satirically exemplified by Jimmie Durham's and Stephen Colbert's respective claims to be male "although only one of my parents was male"[86] or "cis-white" because "I've always been comfortable with my birth race."[87]

The academic efforts to foreground the conventionally unmarked social identities "male," "white," and "straight" have also inspired the essentially analogous attempt to mark and thereby foreground the traditionally unmarked condition of able-bodiedness rather than simply take it for granted.[88] As Simi Linton, for example, explains her conscious decision to refer to the able-bodied as *nondisabled,*

> [t]he use of *nondisabled* . . . is similar to the strategy of marking and articulating "whiteness." The assumed position in scholarship has always been the male, white, nondisabled [as] the default category. . . . [T]hese positions are not only presumptively hegemonic because they are the *assumed universal* stance, as well as the *presumed neutral* or objective stance, but also undertheorized.[89]

When opting to use this term, therefore, one can no longer remain blind to the "taken-for-granted background that goes about unnoticed."[90] Making such a choice, in other words, "means to make the familiar practices of daily life that seem normal, and are often treated as if they are 'natural,' shine through in all their sociality."[91] As such, it actually allows one to "bracket the taken-for-granted status of normalcy"[92] and remind oneself that, after all, it is but a cultural construct.

Part of what helps us take something for granted, as we have seen, is the fact that we tacitly expect it. As we encounter the unexpected, on the other hand, our sense of normality is therefore disrupted, and our hitherto backgrounded tacit expectations and thus also default assumptions are thrust to the foreground.[93] Not surprisingly, therefore, the familiar is likely to enter our awareness particularly "when failure to do or say something has made its continuance as an unquestioned background doubtful."[94] Like the rules of grammar, which we can actually "follow . . . without an explicit knowledge of their content and yet notice a violation immediately,"[95] we usually become explicitly aware of our taken-for-granted assumptions especially when they are disrupted.[96]

Such a seemingly counterintuitive conclusion has in fact led to the introduction of the so-called "breaching experiment," which is specifically designed to foreground the cognitive discomfort we experience when our expectations and therefore also taken-for-granted assumptions are indeed subverted.[97] Originally introduced by Harold Garfinkel and later also utilized by Stanley Milgram, it basically involves the production of experimentally induced assumption reversals. By essentially asking seated subway passengers, "Excuse me. May I have your seat?"[98] or pretending to take acquaintances' merely polite "How are you?"[99] inquiries literally, the experimenter thus manages to make them (as well as the readers of his or her findings) explicitly aware of the default assumptions they tacitly take for granted.

Artistic Foregrounding

Activists and academics, however, are not the only ones who try to subvert prevailing semiotic asymmetries by purposefully foregrounding the conventionally unmarked. So, indeed, do artists.[100] After all, "maintaining the familiar as strange is fundamental to disciplined creativity,"[101] and by "remov[ing] objects from the automatism of perception" art in fact helps make them unfamiliar.[102] In "mak[ing] things the object of attention rather than of habituated action"[103] it thus promotes deautomatization and therefore defamiliarization.

Consider, for example, poetry, aptly characterized by Novalis as "[t]he art . . . of making an object strange,"[104] an idea more explicitly developed later by Shklovsky, who viewed it as specifically designed

> to counteract the process of habituation encouraged by routine everyday modes of perception. We . . . cease to "see" the world we live in. . . . The aim of poetry is to reverse that process, to defamiliarize that with which we are overly familiar, to "creatively deform" the usual, the normal.[105]

The very role of poetry, in other words, is therefore *to foreground by deautomatizing*.[106] Lamenting the fact that "in consequence of the film of familiarity . . . we have eyes, yet see not," Samuel Coleridge, for instance, praised poetry's ability to "awake[n] the mind's attention from the lethargy of custom."[107] More specifically, added Percy Shelley, it "strips the veil of familiarity from the world" by *"mak[ing] familiar objects be as if they were not familiar."*[108]

The role of art in deautomatizing our perception also underlies Bertolt Brecht's vision of the theater's ability to "estrange the familiar, and problematise the self-evident"[109]:

> Before familiarity can turn into awareness *the familiar must be stripped of its inconspicuousness* [and] labelled as something unusual.[110]

> Characters and incidents from ordinary life . . . being familiar, strike us as more or less natural. Alienating them helps to make them seem remarkable to us.[111]

In fact, he specifically characterized such an "alienation effect" as a way of helping the theatrical audience avoid taking ordinary human occurrences for granted[112] by turning the object of their attention from "something ordinary, familiar" into "something peculiar, striking and unexpected."[113]

A somewhat analogous epistemically subversive effect can also be accomplished by turning the theatrical spotlight on the conventionally ignored, as exemplified by Tom Stoppard's play *Rosencrantz and Guildenstern Are Dead*, which, as implied by its very title, essentially revolves around two minor, "background" characters from *Hamlet*.[114] The same overall epistemic goal is likewise accomplished in films featuring habitually ignored "background persons"[115] such as housemaids (*The Help*), butlers (*The Butler*), or backup singers (*20 Feet from Stardom*), as well as in books such as Georges Perec's *An Attempt at Exhausting a Place in Paris*, which simply chronicles a three-day stream of mundane, "infra-ordinary" occurrences as part of a conscious attempt to capture "that which is . . . not noticed, that which has no importance: what happens when nothing happens."[116]

Indeed, that is precisely what many artistic photographers also try to do. In sharp contrast to tourists, who usually gravitate to conventionally marked "attractions,"[117] they often opt to take pictures of their unmarked, "ordinary" surroundings. Furthermore, when taking a picture, they sometimes also try to actually focus their attention on what is conventionally considered mere "background."[118] As one photography professor instructs beginners, "Emphasize the negative space when taking a picture. Learn to see the interval between visual elements as figure. Position your camera in such a way as to make th[at] interval . . . the integral part of your picture."[119]

Similarly, in drawing classes, students are often instructed to be explicitly aware of the unmarked, background-like spaces between conventionally marked thing-like objects. Art educator Betty Edwards, for example, specifically trains her students to actively notice the shapes of the supposedly shape-less "empty" spaces between pieces of furniture in a room.[120] Disputing the unmarked quality conventionally attributed to such so-called "negative" spaces, fellow art instructor Carl Pur-cell likewise insists that they be explicitly delineated.[121] As so spectacularly exemplified by Maurits Escher's *Plane Filling II*, where every single dark figure also doubles as a background for light ones, and vice versa (see figure 5.2), artistic efforts to portray such spaces as anything but empty[122] are the obvious products of such training.

Figure 5.2. Artistic Foregrounding. M. C. Escher's "Plane Filling II" © 2017 The M.C. Escher Company - The Netherlands. All rights reserved. www.mcescher.com

Comic Foregrounding

On January 21, 2008, during his Democratic presidential debate with Hillary Clinton and John Edwards, then-Senator Barack Obama made the following observation about the significance of race in the presidential election that year:

> I think the media, you know, has really been focused a lot on race as we move down to South Carolina. . . . And, I mean, I'm not entirely faulting the media because, look, race is a factor in our society. There's no doubt that in a race where you've got *an African American, and a woman, and*—[a brief, masterfully timed pause]—*John*, there's no doubt that that has piqued interest.[123]

The way he wittily characterized the three remaining Democratic presidential candidates generated a lot of laughter.[124] After all, in sharp contrast to his pronouncedly marked references to both Clinton (*a woman*) and himself (*an African American*), referring to Edwards as simply *John* (a name that also happens to conventionally signify genericity) effectively portrayed him as an ordinary, "plain-vanilla" candidate whose election, unlike that of either Clinton's or Obama's, would be of no great historical significance.

Given the fact that it is often actually based on some fundamental incompatibility with prior expectations (as exemplified by Durham's and Colbert's respective "claims" to be male and "cis-white"), humor helps foreground our habitually taken-for-granted default assumptions by *mocking their presumed normality*. Consider, for example, the following joke:

> PETER: I know one hundred lovemaking positions.
> PAUL: Let's see—there is the one where the man is on top of the woman, the one where . . .

PETER: Oh, right, so I actually know one hundred *and one* positions.

By foregrounding the position conventionally assumed by default (and therefore presumed to have actually been one of the one hundred positions mentioned initially) instead of taking it for granted, the joke essentially mocks its presumed normality.

Consider also the following excerpt from an article titled "Body Ritual among the Nacirema" published in 1956 by Horace Miner in the *American Anthropologist*:

> The Nacirema have an almost pathological . . . fascination with the mouth, the condition of which is believed to have a supernatural influence on all social relationships. Were it not for the rituals of the mouth, they believe that . . . their friends [would] desert them, and their lovers reject them. . . . The daily body ritual performed by everyone includes a mouth-rite [that] involves a practice which strikes the uninitiated stranger as revolting. It was reported to me that the ritual consists of inserting a small bundle of hog hairs into the mouth, along with certain magical powders, and then moving the bundle in a highly formalized series of gestures.[125]

It may have been the realization that *Nacirema* is, after all, *American* spelled backward that led Miner's readers to finally figure out that they were actually reading an allegorical portrayal of their own essentially ordinary oral hygiene practices wittily disguised as some bizarre "Nacirema" rituals. At a time when anthropologists were studying mostly faraway, "exotic" cultures, the last thing those readers expected to be featured in the flagship journal of the American Anthropological Association was a description of their own daily habits. Reading the article must have therefore felt like watching somebody for some time before realizing that one is actually looking in the mirror! By effectively exoticizing the familiar and therefore taken-for-granted, Miner thus tacitly mocked the very acts of abnormalizing and othering, let alone the very notion of normality.

Comic foregrounding often involves the use of both satirical and sarcastic forms of irony. After all, irony constitutes a particularly effective form of social critique, as evidenced by Freeman's aforementioned allusion to "White History Month," by commentator Bret Stephens's tongue-in-cheek suggestion that only a mass deportation of *non*-immigrants can save America,[126] or by the following exchange between Huck and Aunt Sally in Mark Twain's *The Adventures of Huckleberry Finn* acerbically condemning nineteenth-century white America's callous disregard for blacks' lives:

> "It warn't the grounding—that didn't keep us back but a little. We blowed out a cylinder-head."
> "Good gracious! anybody hurt?"
> "No'm. Killed a nigger."
> "Well, it's lucky; because sometimes people do get hurt."[127]

As such, irony is often used to subvert fundamental conventional default assumptions such as andronormativity. Ironic quips such as "Man, being a mammal, breast-feeds his young,"[128] "Menstrual pain accounts for an enormous loss of manpower hours,"[129] or "The university's four-man crews won in both the men's and women's divisions,"[130] for example, thus mock the conventionally presumed genericity of maleness. So, for that matter, does a cartoon showing a little girl standing by a blackboard listing the terms *Stone Age Man*, *Bronze Age Man*, and *Iron Age Man* and asking the teacher, "Did they have women in those days?"[131] or the joke "Did the Enlightenment expand 'the rights of man' . . . ? Yes, but it narrowed the rights of women."[132]

Yet the most spectacular example of the comic subversion of andronormativity is the classic riddle about a fatal car accident in which the man driving the car dies on the spot and his son is rushed to a nearby hospital, where upon seeing him there a startled surgeon exclaims: "I can't operate on my own son!"[133] As Douglas Hofstadter describes this seemingly illogical puzzle,

> What do you make of this grim riddle? How could it be? Was the surgeon lying or mistaken? No. Did the dead father's soul somehow get reincarnated in the surgeon's body? No. Was the surgeon the boy's true father and the dead man the boy's adopted father? No. What then is the explanation?[134]

By far the simplest solution, of course, would be that the surgeon must therefore be the boy's *mother*. Yet as I have come to realize after trying this riddle on friends and students and watching many of them failing to solve it, people often seem to find it difficult to invoke the image of a female surgeon, thereby exposing the taken-for-granted conventional assumption that the term *surgeon* actually implies a man.[135]

Andronormativity is similarly satirized in a Cameron Harvey cartoon showing a nonwhite woman looking in a library for a book on "the white-male experience"[136] (see figure 5.3), yet the cartoon of course also targets leukonormativity. So, indeed, does using the term *Ivorics*, which, by effectively putting the traditionally unmarked "white, caucasian, or anglo manner of speaking"[137] on an equal semiotic footing with so-called "Ebonics," tacitly subverts the conventional racist assumption that only nonwhites use marked, nonstandard, "abnormal" forms of English.

By the same token, by effectively parodying the way white people walk and talk, both Richard Pryor in his skit "White

"Do you have any books on the white-male experience?"

Figure 5.3. Comic Foregrounding. Cameron Harvey/The New Yorker Collection/ The Cartoon Bank

People Eat Quiet"[138] and Eddie Murphy in his skit "White Like Me"[139] tried to subvert the glaring semiotic asymmetry whereby only nonwhites' behavior is conventionally abnormalized, thereby tacitly challenging the presumed normality and therefore taken-for-grantedness of whites' behavior. The epistemically subversive undertones of such humor are also evident in Christian Lander's satirically titled book *Stuff White People Like: The Definitive Guide to the Unique Taste of Millions*[140] as well as in Steve Martin's sarcastic allusion to the fact that, given the way we conventionally attach unmistakably restrictive popular stereotypes only to marked identities, white actors' character repertoire is actually considerably *wider* than that of actors of color:

> The biggest difficulty for me in being white is getting type-cast in mostly white roles. When I first started I guess I should have done more black roles but one picture led to another and pretty soon I was known as a white person. I read for "The Wilt Chamberlain Story" and I was very good but they cast a less-experienced black person in the role. It's one of the things you have to live with as a white person in the United States.[141]

Consider also, along these lines, the essentially analogous ironic subversion of heteronormativity, as so perfectly exemplified by advice columnist Amy Dickinson's tongue-in-cheek response to a mother who feels betrayed by her son's "decision to become" gay:

> DEAR AMY: I recently discovered that my son . . . is a homosexual. We are part of a church group and I fear that if people in that group find out they will make fun of me for having a gay child. . . . I feel as if he is doing this just to get back at me.
>
> DEAR BETRAYED: You could teach your son an important lesson by changing your own sexuality to show him how easy it is. Try it for the next year or so: Stop being a heterosexual to demonstrate to your son that a person's sexuality is a matter of choice.[142]

Such a scathing critique of heteronormativity likewise underlies Charles Moser and Peggy Kleinplatz's satirical article "Does Heterosexuality Belong in the DSM?" which mocks the presumed normality of straightness (effectively featured as a

condition characterized by "recurrent, intense sexually arous-
ing fantasies, sexual urges, or behaviors involving sexual ac-
tivity with an adult of the other sex")[143] with tongue-in-cheek
scientific-sounding statements such as the following:

> Doubts and insecurities about making or keeping relation-
> ship commitments and subsequent attempts to save dam-
> aged or dysfunctional relationships appear to be common
> problems among heterosexuals. . . . [M]any individuals suffer
> endlessly in heterosexual relationships.[144]

The authors sarcastically "concede," however, that "[j]ust because relationship . . . problems are endemic among heterosexuals does not mean that the heterosexuality is the cause of
these problems."[145]

Such epistemically subversive satirical undertones also per-
vade Martin Rochlin's famous "Heterosexual Questionnaire,"[146]
which, effectively lampooning the presumed normality and
therefore taken-for-grantedness of straightness, consists of
tongue-in-cheek questions such as,

> When and how did you first decide you were a heterosexual?
> What do you think caused your heterosexuality?
> Why do you insist on flaunting your heterosexuality?
> Is it possible your heterosexuality is just a phase you may
>   grow out of?
> A disproportionate majority of child molesters are hetero-
>   sexual men. Do you consider it safe to expose children
>   to heterosexual male teachers, pediatricians, priests, or
>   scoutmasters?

Effectively subverting conventional stereotypes, this questionnaire actually "reverses the assumptions . . . that homosexuals
frequently endure."[147] By essentially "reversing the gaze,"[148]

such assumption reversal thus basically turns one of our most fundamental seemingly self-evident default assumptions on its head.

Backgrounding

As we saw above, the simplest and most common form of subverting the fundamental semiotic asymmetry between the marked and the unmarked through altering the relative weights of the two pans of the proverbial scale vis-à-vis each other is by marking the yet unmarked thereby making it semiotically weighty. Yet subverting such asymmetry can in fact be just as effectively accomplished by using the exact opposite form of semiotic "weight management," namely *unmarking the hitherto marked* thereby making it semiotically weightless (see figure 5.4). And as one might expect, whereas marking the yet unmarked involves foregrounding, unmarking the hitherto

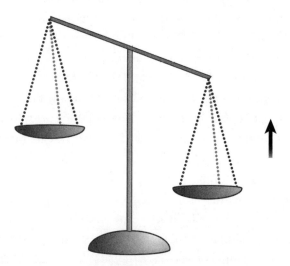

Figure 5.4. Semiotic Subversion II: Unmarking the Hitherto Marked

marked actually involves the diametrically opposite cognitive process of *backgrounding*.[149]

Whereas marking the yet unmarked inevitably involves narrowing its semantic scope, unmarking the hitherto marked actually involves expanding it and thereby increasing its referential potential by making it semiotically less restrictive. That implies making it more vague and thus also more semiotically inclusive. Such vagueness is evident, for example, in the effort to relabel same-sex marriage *equal marriage* as well as in the use of the gender-neutral, "unisex" pronouns *one* (as in *it takes one three hours to complete it*), singular *they* (as in *if someone is born that way, they cannot help it*), or *ze*[150] instead of the gender-specific *he* and *she*. It is likewise exemplified by the functionally analogous politico-semiotic act of replacing traditional job titles such as *policeman, fireman,* and *salesman* with their gender-neutral equivalents *police officer, firefighter,* and *salesperson*.

Furthermore, whereas marking the yet unmarked may also entail narrowing a noun's original semantic scope thereby making it more specific by adding a modifying adjective, unmarking the hitherto marked often involves genericizing and thus "neutralizing" it by *removing an adjective* as part of a conscious effort to make it more vague and therefore semiotically inclusive. "When I was growing up," says Serena Williams, "I had a dream . . . to be the best tennis player in the world. Not the best 'female' tennis player in the world. . . . People call me one of the 'world's greatest female athletes.' Do they say LeBron is one of the world's best *male* athletes? Is Tiger? Federer?"[151] The same semiotic logic, indeed, was also used by Jenn Branson-Scala and Amy Meyers, who both responded to the U. S. Supreme Court's decision to legalize same-sex marriage with the slogan "It's No Longer Gay Marriage. It's Just Marriage,"[152] as well as Anna Brnabić, who on the eve of becoming Serbia's first openly gay prime minister announced, "I don't want to be branded as a gay minister, just as my colleagues don't want to be primarily defined as being straight."[153]

Unmarking the hitherto marked is a necessary part of any attempt to "blend in" in order to attain a certain degree of cultural invisibility.[154] Various "corrective" procedures such as rhinoplasty and "excess" fat removal exemplify such efforts to produce unmarked, "normal" bodies.[155] So, in fact, do immigrants' efforts to shed their marked ethnicity and assume a supposedly generic ethnoracial identity by trying to "neutralize" their accent[156] or wearing jeans.[157] Effectively considered "nondescript," jeans, of course, "don't stand out."[158] As such, they thus constitute unmarked "default clothes" that allow their wearers to avoid undue attention and essentially "achieve ordinariness."[159]

As two diametrically opposed cognitive tactics, foregrounding and backgrounding are both specifically designed to eliminate the fundamental asymmetry between the marked and unmarked regions of our phenomenal world by making the two pans of the aforementioned proverbial scale effectively symmetrical. Using them together complementarily, however, allows us nevertheless to preserve a topsy-turvy (and therefore still semiotically subversive) version of such asymmetry by essentially *backgrounding the hitherto marked while simultaneously foregrounding the yet unmarked*, as respectively illustrated by the right and left arrows in figure 5.5.

Such an epistemically subversive spirit underlies, for example, the following response to the U.S. women's national soccer team's victory in the 2015 World Cup: "After this game, everyone better start calling it 'soccer' and 'men's soccer.'"[160] It likewise underlies Samuel Butler's witty definition of a hen as but "an egg's way of making another egg,"[161] thus effectively

Figure 5.5. Semiotic Subversion III: Foregrounding and Backgrounding Combined

inverting the relations between the conventionally non-agentic and thereby typically backgrounded part of the chicken-and-egg cycle and its conventionally agentic and therefore foregrounded counterpart by essentially foregrounding the former while at the same time backgrounding the latter.

Along somewhat similar lines, consider the following observation made by Jeffrey Olick and his colleagues about the term *collective memory*, the very use of which in fact implies that in its "basic," unmarked form, memory is actually fundamentally personal:

> Because we are sociologists, we believe . . . that if there is such a thing as "memory per se" it is to be found in society. . . . [I]f anyone's enterprise needs an adjective, it is the psychologists who should employ the modifier "individual" to refer to the special case they study, rather than sociologists who should be required to employ the . . . labels

"collective" or "social." . . . [A]s sociologists, we have indeed always begun from the assumption that it is individuality that is the special case requiring philosophical specification, not collectivity.[162]

Such semi-facetious critique, indeed, uses the very same logic used by the late comedian Mitch Hedberg to mock the way we conventionally abnormalize the natural form of corn while effectively normalizing its canned and thus artificial counterpart: "You know how they call corn on the cob 'corn on the cob,' right? But that's how it comes out of the ground, man. They should call that 'corn.' They should call every other version 'corn *off* the cob!'"[163]

As implied in H. G. Wells's story "The Country of the Blind" about an imaginary society where only the main protagonist is sighted,[164] one also encounters such *marking reversals*[165] in the world of fantasy. A perfect example is *Homoworld*,[166] a short film specifically designed as an epistemically subversive "awareness-raising tool"[167] about a society in which *homo*sexuality is the established norm and roadside billboards with slogans such as "*Straight* Bashing Is a Crime. Stomp Out *Hetero*phobia" mock the presumed normality of straightness thereby subverting heteronormativity. So, for that matter, is a formal "dinner" scene in Luis Buñuel's film *The Phantom of Liberty*, in which all the chairs around the "dining" room table are replaced by toilets, and both the hosts and the guests, casually lifting their dresses or dropping their pants, sit down and chat amiably about excrement. Then, after a while, one of the guests pulls up his pants, excuses himself from the table, and goes to a small room down the hall where, locking the door behind him, he sits down by himself and proceeds to eat his dinner. Effectively transposing the semiotic weights we conventionally attach to the supposedly contrasting acts of eating (which, other than on "special" occasions, is by and large culturally unmarked) and defecating (which is considered "private" and, as such, culturally marked), the scene exemplifies the remarkable epistemically subversive potential of such semiotic reversals.

Consider also, along similar lines, Viviana Zelizer's allegorical critique of conventional reward arrangements in the opening paragraph of a scholarly essay about payments and social ties:

> Suppose for a moment that this is the year 2096. . . . "[H]ousewives" and "househusbands" receive monthly stipulated sums of money as salaries from their wage-earning spouses. Salaries are renegotiated yearly; fines imposed for sloppy cleaning, incompetent cooking, careless child care, or indifferent lovemaking. Midyear raises or cash prizes are awarded for exceptional performance. An arbitration board solves domestic financial disputes.[168]

As in *The Phantom of Liberty*, such an epistemically subversive vision of future domestic life is soon complemented by a diametrically contrasting satirical vision of an imagined future workplace where employers reward exceptional performances by occasionally taking workers out to dinner and a movie.[169] Effectively inverting the way we conventionally structure reward in the form of systematic compensation at work yet only random "nice gestures" at home, Zelizer thus challenges the presumed normality of our largely taken-for-granted systems of payment.

Finally, consider also Esther Rothblum's satirical attempt to effectively redistribute the respective semiotic weights culturally attached to romantic and platonic relations by reversing the conventional attribution of markedness to lovers and unmarkedness to "mere" friends:

Whether you have a current Friend and how things are going in your Friendship is the first thing that . . . lovers or family members want to know when they see you.[170]

Scores of how-to books . . . focus on ways to meet a Friend, to "work on" your Friendship, to keep your Friend from leaving you for another, or to keep a longterm Friendship from losing its spice. And everyone knows that the older you are when a Friendship ends, the harder it will be to enter into another Friendship because most people your age already have Friends and are thus "taken."[171]

If you spend too much time with one particular lover, people may wonder whether you are more than "just lovers" and suspect that you are "cheating" on your Friend. You can have fantasies of being friendly with lovers, but you're not supposed to "act on" these feelings without endangering your Friendship.[172]

Envisioning a world in which platonic relations are culturally marked whereas romantic ones effectively remain unmarked, Rothblum thus subverts the way we conventionally apply the label "significant others" only to romantic partners, as if their nonromantic counterparts are not deemed significant enough to warrant special cultural marking. And just as a phrase such as *merely romantic* would most probably sound to us somewhat strange compared to *merely platonic*, her conscious, unmistakably strategic use of odd-sounding phrases such as *just lovers* clearly exemplifies the epistemically subversive potential of the politico-semiotic act of challenging the presumably normal.

6

Language and Cultural Change

[T]he reality of a particular sexuality is dependent on and inseparable from the . . . words we use to describe it. . . . "[H]eterosexuality" and "homosexuality" . . . did not exist, and could not have existed as such, before the words "heterosexual" and "homosexual" . . . were available to describe them.

—Jonathan Katz, *The Invention of Heterosexuality*, viii

Given its fundamentally dynamic nature, culture is constantly in flux, and marking traditions, norms, and conventions indeed vary not only cross-culturally, subculturally, and situationally but also historically. What we mark or leave unmarked thus often changes over time, with major shifts in what we consider "ordinary" or "normal" (and thereby assume by default and take for granted) reflecting major cultural changes.

Thus, for example, in the wake of the sexual revolutions of the past half-century, as "marital intercourse has lost its normative centrality [and the] shame of having an out-of-wedlock child has vastly declined," premarital sex is now essentially taken for granted.[1] By the same token, however, given the increasing destigmatization of same-sex sexuality, less and less people still tend to assume straightness by default.

Consider also, along these lines, *changing assumptions* regarding gender. Women now entering traditionally male professions (medicine, law, engineering), for instance, no longer seem to jeopardize their perceived femininity to the extent they once did. By the same token, whereas a woman's decision not to take her husband's last name was still considered in the 1990s "marked, seen as worthy of comment: she has done something; she has 'kept her own name,'"[2] only a generation later it no longer seems so "special." Furthermore, such changing assumptions regarding gender are in fact also starting to affect even the presumed normality and therefore taken-for-grantedness of cisgenderness.

Markedness shifts often reflect major corresponding shifts in statistical prominence. *As something is becoming more common, it also tends to become less marked, and vice versa.* Given the increasingly declining ratio of smokers to nonsmokers, for example, the social identity "smoker" is clearly becoming more culturally marked.[3] By the same token, given the shrinking size of America's white population relative to its nonwhite counterparts,[4] whiteness is no longer taken for granted. And as exemplified by white nationalists' use of the term *white pride* (very much the way anti-gay activists use the term *straight pride*), it has in fact become the basis of a newly marked social identity.

Underlying such markedness shifts, of course, are fundamental *changes in what is conventionally assumed by default.* Pointing in 1930 to such a major assumption reversal made by the increasingly paranoid young Soviet state, it was in fact Jakobson who first noted the politico-semiotic implications of such shifts: "In the current Soviet press you find the following idea expressed, 'We used to say that everyone who is not against us is with us; now we say that everyone who is not with us is against us.'"[5] Similar changing assumptions regarding immigrants and visitors from the Middle East have likewise led national security hardliners such as Newt Gingrich to even propose that the U. S. government "put all the burden of proof on people coming from those countries to show they are not a danger to us."[6]

Consider also in this regard the recent change from an effectively passive to a pronouncedly active definition of consent in American sexual ethics, as so aptly articulated by New York Governor Andrew Cuomo: "It's not about, 'Did the woman say no before she was attacked?' It's whether or not the woman said yes."[7] The change, in other words, involves a fundamental assumption reversal regarding the very meaning of silence. As Michael Kimmel and Gloria Steinem noted after the passage of California's 2014 "Yes Means Yes" law,

> [u]ntil this bill, the prevailing standard has been "no means no." If she says no . . . then the sex is seen as nonconsensual. That is, it's rape. Under such a standard, the enormous gray area between "yes" and "no" is defined residually as "yes": Unless one hears an explicit "no," consent is implied. "Yes means yes" completely redefines that gray area. *Silence is [no longer] consent; it is the absence of consent.* Only an explicit "yes" can be considered consent.[8]

The fundamental assumption reversals accompanying such major cultural changes are usually manifested lexically.[9] Whereas sixty years ago, for example, housekeeping was married middle-class American women's most common occupation, the very existence today of the term *stay-at-home mom* (along with the waning prominence of its contrasting counterpart *working mom*) certainly attests to the decline in its presumed normality and corresponding increase in its cultural markedness.

When experiencing such cultural changes, we sometimes also mark hitherto unmarked terms so as to differentiate them from some newly introduced contrasting terms. The resulting *retronyms*, as William Saffire observed, are specifically designed to "downdate," that is, "to modify a familiar term in a way that calls attention to its not being the updated version."[10] Soon after the electric guitar was invented, for example, the musical instrument traditionally known simply as *guitar* was thus renamed *acoustic guitar*. By the same token, ever since the introduction of the digital watch, the floppy disk, the electric typewriter, and the laptop computer, what were hitherto thought of simply as "watch," "disk," "typewriter," and "computer" have been conceptually recast as "*analog* watch" "*hard* disk," "*manual* typewriter," and "*desktop* computer." That has, of course, also been true of the "*hardcover* book," the "*forward* slash," and "*regular* coffee" ever since the introduction of the paperback book, the backslash, and decaffeinated coffee.

All these retronyms were, of course, introduced in their present marked form only after having already been tacitly assumed in their traditional unmarked form long before that. Their newly added modifying adjectives (*acoustic, analog, regular*), after all, would have been utterly unnecessary earlier because the very features they now explicitly signify used to be implicitly taken for granted. Terms such as *house phone, tap water, indoor volleyball*, or *live music*, for example, would have been totally redundant and therefore semiotically superfluous, of course, prior to the introduction of the mobile phone, bottled water, beach volleyball, and recorded music.

Markedness shifts sometimes also take the form of full-fledged semiotic reversals that essentially involve marking the yet unmarked while at the same time unmarking the hitherto marked. Thus, for example, whereas in the mid- and late-1990s the name *Bush* was assumed to refer to the former U. S. president while referring to his older son actually involved, by contrast, marking his middle initial ("W."), once the latter became president the situation was effectively reversed—the name *Bush* was assumed to refer to the son, and it was the father's name that was in fact marked (*the first President Bush, Bush the Elder, Bush 41, Bush Senior*) instead. By the same token, whereas the term *hockey* originally referred to a game played on a field, in sharp contradistinction from the one played on an ice rink and accordingly referred to as "*ice* hockey," nowadays it is actually used to refer to the latter, while the former is residually referred to as "*field* hockey."[11] And while when sheep were first introduced to Mexico they were sometimes referred to by the local population as "cotton deer," nowadays it is actually deer who are sometimes referred to there as "wild sheep!"[12]

In fact, even the very meaning of the fundamental semiotic act of marking a yet unmarked term may actually shift over time. The terms *marital rape* and *date rape*, not to mention the explicitly more inclusive *acquaintance rape*, for instance, were originally designed to disabuse people of the erroneous assumption that most rapes are committed by strangers, and thereby foreground the far more common, if more culturally ignored, phenomenon of forced sex committed by an acquaintance. In other words, like the somewhat analogous notion of "*domestic* violence," they were specifically introduced as part of a conscious politico-semiotic effort to expand the semantic scope of the concept "rape" to also include forced sex by spouses, dates, co-workers, family members, neighbors, and friends. Yet the very distinction between marked ("marital," "date," "acquaintance") and unmarked rapes has in fact since introduced yet a new politico-semiotic challenge, having also come to be considered by some as "insulting to rape victims, as it deems their pain and humiliation as less than that of a stranger-rape victim."[13] In other words, just as when qualifying tax fraud or embezzlement as merely "*white-collar* crimes" and attacks on computer systems as "*cyber*terrorism," marking certain forms of rape as "marital," "date," or "acquaintance" has over time also come to be viewed as tacitly minimizing the perceived severity of the offense, effectively trivializing it as "rape lite."[14]

Living, as we do, at a time of unprecedentedly rapid cultural change, it might be useful to remind ourselves that the very notion of an "analog" (in contradistinction to a "digital") watch is but a few decades old, and that only a couple of generations ago, for that matter, the very idea that "straight" might one day be considered a full-fledged social identity would have been utterly inconceivable. After all, given the conventional self-evidence of heteronormativity, the very notion of straightness would have been considered culturally redundant and, as such, semiotically superfluous.

Given the unmistakably fluid nature of "normality,"[15] what we consider culturally redundant and therefore semiotically superfluous is historically contingent. And so, indeed, are our very notions of what is considered marked or unmarked. Over the next few decades, let alone centuries, therefore, we can in fact expect considerable changes in what we come to assume by default.

In light of all this, there is absolutely no way of predicting what will be taken for granted a hundred or even twenty years from now! There may very well come a time, for example, when classroom rather than online college courses would be the marked ones, when Goya food products would no longer be displayed in a separate aisle in American supermarkets, and when remaining tattooless or even conforming to one's assigned gender at birth would actually involve making an active, effectively marked identity choice. Furthermore, as one might expect, it is also practically impossible to envision now any of the yet-nonexistent future concepts that are one day going to fill the countless yet-unmarked gaps in our collective imagination.

In fact, I even expect some of the specific examples I use in the book to be somewhat "dated" by the time you read it, yet at the same time strongly believe that the general sociosemiotic patterns they exemplify will nevertheless remain constant. While our view of any particular semiotic object as marked or unmarked may indeed be only ephemeral, the very distinction between the "special" and the "ordinary" is here to stay.

Notes

Preface

1. See, for example, Whorf 1956 [1940].
2. Zerubavel 1989 [1985], 115, 117, 119–20, 136.
3. See, for example, Y. Zerubavel 1995, 8.
4. Zerubavel 2004.
5. Zerubavel 2003, 26–34.
6. Foster 1996; Mullaney 1999; Brekhus 1996; Brekhus 1998; Brekhus 2003.
7. Zerubavel 1997, 1. See also 74–75.
8. Zerubavel 2011, 3. See also 62–64.
9. Zerubavel 2015.

Chapter 1. The Marked and the Unmarked

1. Brekhus 2003, 12.
2. See also Milgram 1992 [1978], 37; Brekhus 2003, 14; Turner 2014, 1.
3. Jakobson and Waugh 2002 [1979], 93; Jakobson and Pomorska 1983 [1980], 95; Andersen 1989, 21. See also Trubetzkoy 1969 [1939].
4. Andersen 1989, 22.
5. Jakobson 1972, 76. Emphasis added. See also Jakobson and Pomorska 1983 [1980], 97.
6. Jakobson and Pomorska 1983 [1980], 95.
7. Waugh 1982, 309–10.
8. On the latter, see Jaszczolt 2005.
9. Foster 1996, 542–43.
10. Hartigan 2005, 316–17.
11. Wray 2006. See also Hartigan 2005, 25, 115, 135, 148, 150.
12. Hofmann 1993, 21.
13. Romaine 1999, 131.
14. See also Brekhus 1998, 35.
15. Google search done on August 20, 2015.
16. Google search done on August 26, 2015.

17. Google search done on October 10, 2016.
18. Google searches done on November 15 and October 10, 2016.
19. On collective attention, see Zerubavel 2015, 69–71.
20. Ibid. 22–23. See also Garfinkel 1967 [1964]; Greenberg 1966, 60; Stalnaker 1973, 447; Kuipers 1975, 43; Waugh 1982, 302; Hundeide 1985; Andersen 1989, 39–40; Battistella 1990, 4–5; Givón 1990, 947–48; Brekhus 2003, 13; Urciuoli 2011, E113; Miller and Woodward 2012, 3.
21. Zerubavel 2015.
22. On those, see Zerubavel 1997.
23. See also Brekhus 1998.
24. Perec 1997 [1973], 206.
25. Nietzsche 1974 [1887], 301.
26. Birenbaum and Sagarin 1973, 3. See also Blank 2012, xvi.
27. Miller and Woodward 2012, 3.
28. For some notable exceptions, see Chambers 1996; Brekhus 1998.
29. On mental blind spots, see Zerubavel 2015, 6, 10, 71; Friedman (forthcoming).
30. See also Tin 2012 [2008], vii.
31. Jakobson 1972, 76; Jakobson and Pomorska 1983 [1980], 95, 97. See also Trubetzkoy 1969 [1939]; Waugh 1976, 90; Jakobson and Waugh 2002 [1979], 93; Andersen 1989, 21; Trubetzkoy 2001, 160; Martella 2010, 429.
32. Hockey et al. 2007, 8.
33. See also Chandler 2007, 145.
34. For two notable exceptions, see Garfinkel 1967 [1964] and Brekhus 1998.
35. Katz 2007 [1995], 16–17.
36. Ibid.

Chapter 2. Semiotic Asymmetry

1. See, for example, Hertz 1973 [1909].
2. See also Battistella 1990, 1, 25, 28, 73.
3. Jakobson and Pomorska 1983 [1980], 97; Andersen 1989, 21; Trubetzkoy 2001, 160. See also Greenberg 1966, 14; Waugh 1976, 90; Givón 1990, 946; Battistella 1990, 25; Givón 1995, 26.
4. Google searches done on December 10, 2016 and December 17, 2016.
5. Mullaney 1999. See also Bonilla-Silva 2012.
6. Wojcik 2015.
7. Mullaney 1999.
8. See also Brekhus 2003.
9. See also Brekhus et al. 2010, 64.
10. Mullaney 1999, 273–75; Mullaney 2006, 5.
11. See also Mullaney 1999, 272–73.

12. See also Battistella 1990, 192.

13. Zerubavel 2011, 62–64, 101–03.

14. See also Schutz, 1967 [1932], 74; Schutz 1973 [1955], 326; Ostrow 1990, 24.

15. Schutz 1973 [1955], 326.

16. See also Bourdieu, 1977 [1972], 164–67.

17. Schutz 1964 [1946], 124. See also Schutz 1973 [1951], 74.

18. See also Ostrow 1990, 13.

19. Schutz and Luckmann 1973, 109. See also Bourdieu 1990 [1980], 53; Ostrow 1990, 29–30.

20. See also Huang 2012, 83.

21. Bourdieu 1977 [1972], 166–67; Bourdieu 1984 [1979], 424; Tannen 1993.

22. Google search done on December 13, 2016.

23. Haspelmath 2006, 26, 36–37.

24. Misztal 2001, 314.

25. See also Levinson 2000, 6.

26. See, for example, Goffman 1971, 283; Erikson 1976; Zerubavel 1985 [1981], 15, 20–30; Halfacree 2014; Francis 2015.

27. Pagliai 2011, E98.

28. Ryan 2006, 241.

29. See also Greenberg 1966, 21; Harris 1973; Waugh 1976, 89; Lyons 1977, 307; Jakobson and Pomorska 1983 [1980], 97; Waugh 1982, 301; Shapiro 1983, 16; Newfield and Waugh 1991 [1985], 227; Battistella 1990, 4, 56; Battistella 1996, 57; Levinson 2000, 115; Andersen 2001, 50; Elšík and Matras 2006, 17; Haspelmath 2006, 29; Holleman and Pander Maat 2009, 2209.

30. Lakoff 1987, 60.

31. Clark 1969, 389. See also Greenberg 1966, 26, 53; Harris 1973, 399; Lyons 1977, 308; Clark and Clark 1977, 427; Battistella, 1990, 3.

32. See also Greenberg 1966, 21; Andersen 2001, 50.

33. Battistella 1996, 56. See also 37–38; Lyons 1977, 306; Newfield and Waugh 1991 [1985], 227.

34. See also Zerubavel 2015, 23.

35. See also Greenberg 1966, 14, 33; Kuipers 1975, 43; Givón 1990, 947; Givón 1995, 25; Brekhus 1998, 35; Haspelmath 2006, 33.

36. Durkheim 1982 [1895], 91–92, 104.

Chapter 3. Social Variations on a Theme

1. Simpson 1996, 553–55.

2. Ibid., 556.

3. Hundeide 1985, 311. Emphasis added.

4. Durkheim 1973 [1914]; Zerubavel 1997, 7–8.

5. See also Schutz 1973 [1955], 327.

6. Woody Allen, "Summing Up," http://www.ibras.dk/comedy/allen.htm (accessed on November 25, 2015).
7. Baum 2010, 31. Emphasis added.
8. Ibid., 32.
9. Brekhus 2015, 43.
10. See, for example, Holleman and Pander Maat 2009, 2204–5.
11. See also Brekhus et al., 2010, 65; Zerubavel 2011, 62–64.
12. Zerubavel 2016, 73.
13. See also Zerubavel 2015, 89–92.
14. See also Zerubavel 1997, 9.
15. See also ibid., 1–22.
16. See, for example, Alpher 1987. See also Shapiro 1982, 718n3.
17. See, for example, Otto et al. 2014.
18. Durkheim 1982 [1895], 100.
19. See, for example, Grazian 2015, 68.
20. Zerubavel 1989 [1985], 26, 114–15.
21. See also ibid., 89.
22. Rachel Brekhus, personal communication.
23. See, for example, Perry 2002.
24. Andersen 1972, 45.
25. Miller and Woodward 2012, 115. Emphasis added.
26. See, for example, Lerner 2015 (accessed on May 21, 2015).
27. Chozick 2015.
28. Bruni 2015b.
29. Petulla 2016; Lewis and Djupe 2016 (accessed on December 23, 2016); Stack 2016; McGill 2016.
30. Amalia Hubal, personal communication.
31. Yancy and Butler 2015 (accessed on July 28, 2015). Emphases added.
32. Brazile 2015 (accessed on July 28, 2015). Emphasis added.
33. Ibid. Emphases added.

Chapter 4. The Politics of Normality

1. See also Beauvoir 1953 [1949], xviii; Tajfel 1981 [1978], 310.
2. See also Trechter and Bucholtz 2001, 5; Chandler 2007, 96, 252; Sasson-Levy and Shoshana 2013, 469.
3. Doane 1997, 378, 380.
4. On these three branches of semiotics, see, for example, Morris 1971 [1938].
5. See also Bodine 1975, 133.
6. Fasold 1990, 114. See also Reynolds et al. 2006, 888.
7. Keller 2000, 40.

8. See, for example, Livia 2001, 82.
9. Kipling 1907, vol. 2, p. 27. Emphasis added.
10. On race as a particular form of ethnicity, see Zerubavel 2011, 57, 153n27.
11. See also Manning 2004, 92–93.
12. See also Kiesling 2007, 654.
13. Warner 1991.
14. See also Martin 2009, 190.
15. Morris 2013.
16. See also Zerubavel 2007.
17. See also Hockey et al. 2007, 11.
18. Maugham 1915, 644.
19. Francis 2015, 12. Emphasis added. See also 131–32.
20. See also Best 2004, 17–18.
21. See also Warner 1999, 56.
22. Poovey 1998, 374.
23. Fiedler 1996 [1984], 154. See also Dudley-Marling and Gurn, 2010.
24. Poovey 1998, 374.
25. Warner 1999, 53.
26. Kinsey et al. 1948, 199.
27. Ibid. 201.
28. See also Comrie 1976, 111; Levinson 2000, 136; Haspelmath 2006, 30, 33.
29. See also Hundeide 1985, 311; Chambers 1996, 142; Titchkosky 2009, 46.
30. Garland-Thomson 1997, 6–7.
31. Heath 2013, 562. See also 573–74.
32. Shapiro 1982, 719n4.
33. Brod 1997, 54.
34. Shapiro 1982, 719n4.
35. Urciuoli 1996, 16.
36. Moore 2005 [1976], 123; Frankenberg 1993, 204; Chambers 1996, 151; Babb 1998, 179; Gabriel 1998, 13; Perry 2001, 57, 59–60; Doane 2003, 7; Dean 2014, 43.
37. Robinson 2000, 14–15. See also Frankenberg 1993, 198.
38. Matsuda 1991, 1361. Emphases added.
39. See, for example, Lippi-Green 1997, 53–62; Urciuoli 1996, 2, 106–07, 118–21; Labov 1972 [1969].
40. Robinson 2000, 1. See also 14–15; Matsuda 1991, 1361.
41. Bucholtz 1999, 443.
42. See also Shapiro 1983, 17–18, 79; Levinson 2000, 115; Elšík and Matras 2006, 17.
43. See also Clark 1969, 390; Givón 1990, 947; Givón 1995, 30; Haspelmath 2006, 26.

44. See also Greenberg 1966, 22–23; Lakoff 1987, 60; Frank and Treichler 1989, 206; Trechter and Bucholtz 2001, 4; Motschenbacher 2010, 94; Urciuoli 2011, E119.
45. Tannen 1993.
46. See also Chandler 2007, 95.
47. Google search done on March 1, 2016.
48. Google searches done on May 3, 2016, and March 15, 2016.
49. See also Heath 2013, 574.
50. Brekhus 1998, 35. See also figure 2 in Brekhus 1996, 501.
51. Blank 2012, 32. Emphasis added. See also Brekhus 1996, 501–03.
52. On moral attention, see Zerubavel 1997, 39–40, 47; Zerubavel 2015, 52, 59.
53. Brekhus 1998, 37.
54. Ibid.
55. See, for example, Cerulo 2006.
56. Durkheim 1995 [1912], 36.
57. See, for example, Davis 1995, 24–30; Garland-Thomson 1997, 63.
58. Quetelet 1842 [1835]. See also Davis 1995, 26; Garland-Thomson 1997, 63; Horwitz 2016, 6.
59. Zerubavel 1997; Zerubavel (forthcoming).
60. See, for example, Foucault 1979 [1975]; Foucault 2003 [1975].
61. See also Brekhus 1996, 497; Bucholtz 1999, 443; Chandler 2007, 96, 98, 252–53, 255; Dolmage and Lewiecki-Wilson 2010, 24.
62. See also Zerubavel 2016, 73–74.
63. Chandler 2007, 96.
64. Hegel 2003 [1807].
65. Brod 1997, 54. See also Tavris 1992, 17; Bem 1993, 2.
66. Misztal 2015, 6.
67. Spivak 1985, 252, 255.
68. See, for example, Erikson 1966; Cohen 1972. See also Dixon 2003, 55.
69. Graham 2002, 39. See also Shepard 1978, 100–03.
70. Garland-Thomson 1997, 77.
71. Goffman 1963b. See also Linton 1998, 5–6.
72. See, for example, Garland-Thomson 1997, 55–80.
73. Ibid., 7. Emphasis added.
74. See, for example, DeGloma 2014.
75. Garland-Thomson 2002, 11. Emphases added. See also Galotti 2016.
76. Garland-Thomson 2002, 12.
77. Brekhus 1998, 35.
78. Google search done on March 14, 2016.
79. See also Bhattacharya 2011.
80. Said 1979.
81. Hockey et al. 2007, 25.

82. Eliason 1996, 73; Kitzinger 2005b, 255, 257.
83. Google search done on February 26, 2017. See also Baker 2008, 115–16.
84. Bruni 2015a.
85. Ibid.
86. Zerubavel 2015.
87. http://www.cnn.com/2008/POLITICS/10/21/palin.sitroom/index.html. Emphasis added.
88. Coulter 2014 (accessed on June 30, 2014). Emphases added.
89. See also Babb 1998, 149, 151; Gabriel 1998, 13; Perry 2001, 59; Dean 2014, 43.
90. Urciuoli 2011, E121. See also E120.
91. See also Zerubavel 2011, 108.
92. See, for example, Ignatiev 1995; Roediger 2005; Goldstein 2006.
93. See, for example, Tuan 1999, 39, 155, 157; Zhou 2004, 35.
94. Calaprice 2010, 10.
95. See, for example, Murphy 2011.
96. See also Brekhus 1996, 519; Brekhus 1998, 41.
97. See also Eichler et al. 1992, 63–65.
98. See also Brekhus 1996, 519.
99. McIntosh 1989, 11.
100. Brekhus 1998, 37. See also Wise 1999.
101. See also Waugh 1982, 309.
102. Listen, for example, to the interview with Dylan Marron on WNYC's "Leonard Lopate Show," August 20, 2015.
103. https://twitter.com/jk_rowling/status/678888094339366914 (accessed on September 20, 2016).
104. See also Clark 1969, 389; Clark and Clark 1977, 427; Garland-Thomson 1997, 8–9; Brekhus 1998, 35; Chandler 2007, 96; Hockey et al. 2007, 1; Dolmage and Lewiecki-Wilson 2010, 24.
105. Bem 1993, 41. See also 2, 145.
106. See also Shepelak 1976, 90–91; Martyna 1980, 489; Silveira 1980, 165; Shapiro 1983, 16; Khosroshahi 1989, 506.
107. Google search done on April 2, 2017.
108. Google searches done on March 9, 2016, and May 6, 2016. See also Katz 2007 [1995], 16.
109. See also Brod 1997, 54.
110. Frankenberg 1993, 205.
111. Urciuoli 1996, 16. See also Moore 2002, 63.
112. See also Dyer 1997, 46.
113. Ibid., 47.
114. See also Trechter and Bucholtz 2001, 5; Zerubavel 2011, 63.
115. Blank 2012, 32. Emphasis added. See also Doane 2003, 7.

116. Moore 2002, 63.
117. Terry 1981, 120. Emphasis added. See also Waters 1990; Perry 2001; Doane 2003, 8.
118. Urciuoli 1996, 16–17.
119. Lieberson 1985.
120. Zhou 2004, 35. Emphasis added.
121. Babb 1998, 161.
122. Doane 1997, 381.
123. Dean 2014, 26.
124. Perry 2002, 96.
125. See also Perry 2001, 57–58, 85; Perry 2002; Doane 2003, 7.
126. See also Minnich 2005, 95.
127. Google search done on March 9, 2016.
128. See also Motschenbacher 2010, 29.
129. See also Zerubavel 2015, 27–28.
130. Doane 2003, 17.
131. See also Robinson 2000, 1, 194.
132. Frankenberg 1993, 6; Doane 1997, 377–78; Garland-Thomson 1997, 40; Dyer 1997, 45; McDermott and Samson 2005, 248.
133. Frankenberg 1993, 228; Doane 1997, 378; Brod 1997, 54; Frankenberg 2001, 73, 77; Frankenberg 2004, 116.
134. Sasson-Levy 2013, 36.
135. Ibid. Emphasis added.
136. Frankenberg 1993, 196–97.
137. See also Simpson and Lewis 2005, 1263, 1270; Chandler 2007, 96.
138. Simpson and Lewis 2005, 1263.
139. See also Doane 1997, 384; Ergun 2010, 311.
140. See also Collinson and Hearn 1994.
141. Blank 2012, 164. See also Hockey et al. 2007, 5.
142. Hockey et al. 2007, 126. See also Jackson 2005, 23.
143. Dean 2014, 32. Emphasis added. See also Kitzinger 2005b.
144. See also Haraway 1989, 152; Doane 1997, 384; Robinson 2000, 194.
145. Dean 2014, 43.
146. See also Sasson-Levy and Shoshana 2013, 455, 463.
147. Doane 1997, 377–78.
148. See also Bhabha 1994 [1992], 171.
149. Spence 1978, 9, 173, 183, 219–20. See also Zerubavel 1997, 17; Zerubavel 2006, 38; DeGloma 2007; Genieys and Smyrl 2008, 11, 22, 27, 171; Friedman 2013, 34–46; Zerubavel 2015, 62.
150. See also Hofstadter 1985 [1982], 137.
151. See also Caffi 1997, 439.

152. See also Bourdieu 1977 [1972], 164–67; Simon-Vandenbergen et al. 2007, 58–65.
153. Givón 2001, 327. See also Sbisà 1999, 501.
154. See also Gramsci 1995, 290–91.
155. See also Zerubavel 2016.
156. Warner 1999, 60.

Chapter 5. Semiotic Subversion

1. Brekhus 1998, 43–45.
2. Mahler 2016, A18.
3. Kuhn 1970 [1962], 85, 111–14, 150. See also Zerubavel 2015, 83.
4. Horowitz 2012. Emphasis added.
5. Zerubavel 2006, 65–68; Zerubavel 2015, 82–89.
6. See, for example, Friedman 2013, 110.
7. Zerubavel 2015, 23.
8. See also Brekhus 1996, 518.
9. Brown 1984, 154–56.
10. Christine Galotti, personal communication. See also Zerubavel 2015, 67, 77, 85, 93.
11. Zerubavel 2015.
12. Fingarette 1969, 45. See also 39.
13. Beiser 1998, 294. Emphasis added. See also O'Brien 1995, 317; Robinson 2008, 79–80.
14. Shklovsky 1965 [1917]. See also Ornstein 2008 [1971], 61–76; Van Peer 1986, 1–5; Miall and Kuiken 1994, 391.
15. Gordon 1961, 34.
16. See, for example, DiMaggio 1997, 271–72.
17. Deikman 1966. See also Shklovsky 1965 [1917]; Ornstein 2008 [1971], 61–76; Van Peer 1986, 2; Kabat-Zinn 1990, 21–22.
18. Deikman 1966, 329; Robinson 2008, 98. See also Shklovsky 1965 [1917], 11; Havránek 1964 [1932], 11.
19. See also Ybema and Kamsteeg 2009, 108.
20. See also Polanyi 1966.
21. Larson 2003 [March 19, 1992], 393.
22. See also Zerubavel 2006, 64–68.
23. See, for example, Bonilla-Silva 2012.
24. https://www.youtube.com/watch?v=GeixtYS-P3s (accessed on June 24, 2016).
25. Wise 1999.
26. Ibid.

27. https://www.youtube.com/watch?v=OdSsBYO1oNI (accessed on April 22, 2017).
28. Robinson 2000, 25, 17.
29. Ibid., 16.
30. See also Gervis 2015. On foregrounding the invisible, see also Zerubavel 2006, 65–68; Zerubavel 2015, 82–89.
31. Dunn 2012 (accessed on July 28, 2017); Gervis 2015.
32. See also Brekhus 1998, 45.
33. MacKinnon 1979, 27. See also Whorf 1956 [1940].
34. See also Zerubavel 2006, 65, 73–74; Zerubavel 2015, 84.
35. Kelly 1988, 139.
36. Joy 2010.
37. See, for example, Cole and Morgan 2011.
38. Ryder 1989.
39. See also Kelly 1988, 139.
40. Katz 2007 [1995], 154, 158–59.
41. Beaver 1981, 115.
42. Linton 1998, 13.
43. Ndopu 2013.
44. Linton 1998, 13–14, 24; Titchkosky 2003, 13.
45. Katz 2007 [1995], 95.
46. See, for example, Davis 1995, 1, 7, 172.
47. Whitehead and Whitehead 2014, 74. See also Whyte and Ingstad 1995, 4.
48. See also Hockey et al. 2007, 1–2.
49. Davis 1995, xv.
50. See, for example, Rubin 2002 [1984], 202.
51. See also Wouters 2002 [1998], 49.
52. See, for example, Aultman 2014, 61.
53. Koyama 2013 [2002] (accessed on September 20, 2016).
54. Aultman 2014, 62.
55. See, for example, Zerubavel 1980, 29–30, 32; Myers 2011. See also James 1911, 7.
56. Proust 2006 [1923], 657. See also Fleck 1979 [1935], 82–145; Kuhn 1970 [1962].
57. Tavory and Timmermans 2014, 55.
58. Hall 1969 [1966]. See also Zerubavel 1997, 46.
59. See, for example, Goffman 1963a; Goffman 1971.
60. Goffman 1971, 260. See also Brekhus 1998; Horowitz 2013.
61. Coffey 2004, 21. Emphasis added. See also Delamont and Atkinson 1995, 3, 7, 147.
62. Gronow and Warde 2001, 4.

63. Micciche 2010, 176. Emphasis added.
64. See, for example, Tannen 1993; Ergun 2010, 311.
65. See also Shapiro 1982, 720.
66. Collinson and Hearn 1994, 5.
67. See, for example, Doane 2003.
68. See also Dyer 1997, 13.
69. Frankenberg 2004, 104. See also 112.
70. Lippi-Green 1997, 41–52.
71. Ibid., 43.
72. Ibid., xiv.
73. Horwitz 2016, 184. Emphasis added.
74. Kitzinger 2005a, 478.
75. Rich 1980.
76. Ingraham 2005.
77. Blank 2012.
78. Dean 2014.
79. Tin 2012 [2008].
80. Kitzinger 2005a, 478.
81. Katz 2007 [1995], 9. Emphasis added.
82. Wilkinson and Kitzinger 1993.
83. Blank 2012, 33.
84. Heath 2013, 564.
85. Brod 2002, 166–67.
86. Strong and van Winkle 1996, 551.
87. Steinmetz 2014 (accessed on September 20, 2016).
88. See also McRuer 2006, 1–32.
89. Linton 1998, 13–14. Emphasis added. See also 24.
90. Titchkosky 2003, 19.
91. Ibid.
92. Ibid., 157.
93. See, for example, Goffman 1971, 238–333; Erikson 1976; Zerubavel 1985 [1981]: 22–26; Halfacree 2014; Francis 2015.
94. Birenbaum and Sagarin 1973, 9.
95. Milgram 1992 [1978], 37.
96. Carroll 1990, 133.
97. Rogers 1981, 147.
98. Milgram 1992 [1978], 39–40.
99. Garfinkel 1967 [1964], 44.
100. See also Chandler 2007, 70.
101. Gordon 1961, 36.
102. Shklovsky 1965 [1917], 13, 12.

103. Tavory and Timmermans 2014, 56.
104. O'Brien 1995, 317.
105. Hawkes 1977, 62. See also Amsterdam and Bruner 2000, 4.
106. Mukařovský 1964 [1932], 19. See also Havránek 1964 [1932], 10.
107. Coleridge 1983 [1817], vol. 2, p. 7.
108. Shelley 1840, 58, 35. Emphasis added.
109. Brooker 2006 [1994], 223. See also Eriksson 2011, 67.
110. Willett 1992, 144. Emphasis added.
111. Ibid., 140.
112. Ibid., 125. See also Bundy et al. 2013, 146.
113. Willett 1992, 143.
114. Stoppard 1967.
115. Zerubavel 2015, 28–30.
116. Perec 1975, 3. See also Horowitz 2013.
117. See, for example, MacCannell 1999 [1976].
118. See Zerubavel 2015.
119. Zakia 2002, 21.
120. Edwards 1979, 102–09; Edwards 1999, 116–35. See also Ehrenzweig 1953, 28, 36.
121. Purcell 2010, 141–42.
122. See also Zerubavel 2015, 86–89, plates 4, 5, and 6.
123. http://www.presidency.ucsb.edu/ws/index.php?pid=76271 (accessed on May 20, 2015), emphasis added; 0:54 at https://www.youtube.com/watch?v=KghL5py60f8 (accessed on May 20, 2015).
124. See 1:37 at https://www.youtube.com/watch?v=KghL5py60f8 (accessed on May 20, 2015).
125. Miner 1956, 504.
126. Stephens 2017.
127. Twain 1961 [1885], 173 (chapter 32).
128. Martyna 1980, 489.
129. Ibid. See also Romaine 1999, 102.
130. Fasold 1990, 111.
131. Romaine 1999, 103.
132. Tavris 1992, 18.
133. This riddle was featured on the "Gloria and the Riddle" episode of *All in the Family* on October 7, 1972 (and in 1988 also on *The Cosby Show*).
134. Hofstadter 1985 [1982], 136.
135. See also ibid., 136–37; Reynolds et al. 2006, 889.
136. *The New Yorker*, August 3, 2015, p. 51.
137. http://www.urbandictionary.com/define.php?term=ivorics (accessed on May 19, 2015).

138. https://www.youtube.com/watch?v=AOwVSgs3Gbg (accessed on May 25, 2015).

139. http://www.rollingstone.com/tv/pictures/50-greatest-saturday-night -live-sketches-of-all-time-20140203/white-like-me-0201086 (accessed on May 26, 2015).

140. Lander 2008.

141. Davis 1993, 180.

142. Dickinson 2013 (accessed on July 19, 2015).

143. Moser and Kleinplatz 2005, 262.

144. Ibid., 264.

145. Ibid., 265.

146. https://www.uwgb.edu/pride-center/files/pdfs/Heterosexual _Questionnaire.pdf (accessed on June 27, 2015).

147. Morin and Kimmel 2004, 958.

148. Seymour-Smith 2015, 317.

149. Zerubavel 2015, 45–46.

150. See, for example, Weber 2014.

151. Williams 2016. https://www.theguardian.com/lifeandstyle/2016/nov /29/dream-big-open-letter-serena-williams-porter-magazine-incredible -women-of-2016-issue-women-athletes (accessed on April 22, 2017). Emphasis added.

152. See, for example, http://thecourier.com/breaking-news/2015/06/26 /wood-county-will-issue-same-sex-marriage-licenses-today/ (accessed on June 29, 2015); http://www.news-gazette.com/news/local/2015-06 -27/courts-ruling-makes-glorious-day.html (accessed on June 29, 2015). See also Harper 2012 (accessed on June 11, 2016).

153. Surk 2017. On "attentional battles" over relevance see also Zerubavel 2015, 57.

154. See, for example, Force 2010. See also Zerubavel 2015, 27–44.

155. See also Garland-Thomson 2002, 11; Galotti 2016.

156. See also Aneesh 2015, 57–62.

157. Miller and Woodward 2012, 105–06.

158. Ibid., 96, 91. See also 87–88, 90.

159. Ibid., 84, 101.

160. https://twitter.com/jaclynf/status/617835123317317632 (accessed on July 6, 2015).

161. Butler 2013 [1878], 116.

162. Olick et al. 2014, 134–35.

163. http://en.wikipedia.org/wiki/Mitch_All_Together (accessed on May 27, 2015). Emphasis added.

164. Wells 1978 [1904].

165. See also Andersen 1972, 45; Witkowski and Brown 1983.
166. https://www.youtube.com/watch?v=HJXw8PthD0M (accessed on June 12, 2016).
167. Butler 2004, 15.
168. Zelizer 1996, 481–82.
169. Ibid., 482.
170. Rothblum 1999, 72.
171. Ibid., 73.
172. Ibid., 72.

Chapter 6. Language and Cultural Change

1. Horwitz 2016, 191.
2. Tannen 1993.
3. See also Zerubavel 1997, 44; Zerubavel 2015, 58.
4. See also McDermott and Samson 2005, 245, 248.
5. Roman Jakobson, in Andersen 1989, 22.
6. Healy and Barbaro 2015, A19.
7. Tcholakian 2015.
8. Kimmel and Steinem 2014. Emphasis added.
9. Witkowski and Brown 1983.
10. Safire 1992.
11. Millar and Trask 2015, 34.
12. Witkowski and Brown 1983, 571.
13. Fields and Kirchoff 2011, 80.
14. Dirks and Troshynski 2016, 508.
15. See also Canguilhem 1991 [1966], 174.

Bibliography

Alpher, Barry. "Feminine as the Unmarked Grammatical Gender: Buffalo Girls Are No Fools." *Australian Journal of Linguistics* 7 (1987): 169–87.

Amsterdam, Anthony G., and Jerome S. Bruner. *Minding the Law*. Cambridge, MA: Harvard University Press, 2000.

Andersen, Henning. "Dipthongization." *Language* 48 (1972): 11–50.

———. "Markedness Theory: The First 150 Years." In Olga Mišeska Tomić (ed.), *Markedness in Synchrony and Diachrony*, 11–46. Berlin: Mouton De Gruyter, 1989.

———. "Markedness and the Theory of Linguistic Change." In Henning Andersen (ed.), *Actualization: Linguistic Change in Progress*, 21–57. Amsterdam: John Benjamins, 2001.

Aneesh, A. *Neutral Accent: How Language, Labor, and Life Become Global*. Durham, NC: Duke University Press, 2015.

Aultman, B. "Cisgender." *TSQ: Transgender Studies Quarterly* 1 (2014): 61–62.

Babb, Valerie. *Whiteness Visible: The Meaning of Whiteness in American Literature and Culture*. New York: New York University Press, 1998.

Baker, Paul. *Sexed Texts: Language, Gender, and Sexuality*. London: Equinox, 2008.

Battistella, Edwin L. *Markedness: The Evaluative Superstructure of Language*. Albany: State University of New York Press, 1990.

———. *The Logic of Markedness*. New York: Oxford University Press, 1996.

Baum, Dan. "Happiness Is a Worn Gun: My Concealed Weapon and Me." *Harper's Magazine*, August 2010, pp. 29–38.

Beauvoir, Simone de. *The Second Sex*. New York: Alfred A. Knopf, 1953 [1949].

Beaver, Harold. "Homosexual Signs: In Memory of Roland Barthes." *Critical Inquiry* 8 (1981): 99–119.

Beiser, Frederick C. "A Romantic Education: The Concept of *Bildung* in Early German Romanticism." In Amélie O. Rorty (ed.), *Philosophers on Education*, 284–99. London: Routledge, 1998.

Bem, Sandra L. *The Lenses of Gender: Transforming the Debate on Sexual Inequality*. New Haven, CT: Yale University Press, 1993.

Best, Joel. "Theoretical Issues in the Study of Social Problems and Deviance." In George Ritzer (ed.), *Handbook of Social Problems: A Comparative International Perspective*, 14–29. Thousand Oaks, CA: SAGE Publications, 2004.

Bhabha, Homi K. "The Postcolonial and the Postmodern." In *The Location of Culture*, 171–97. London: Routledge, 1994 [1992].

Bhattacharya, Usree. "The 'West' in Literacy." *Berkeley Review of Education* 2 (2011): 179–98.

Birenbaum, Arnold, and Edward Sagarin. "Introduction: Understanding the Familiar." In *People in Places: The Sociology of the Familiar*, 3–11. New York: Praeger, 1973.

Blank, Hanne. *Straight: The Surprisingly Short History of Heterosexuality*. Boston: Beacon Press, 2012.

Bodine, Ann. "Androcentrism in Prescriptive Grammar: Singular 'They,' Sex-Indefinite 'He,' and 'He or She.'" *Language in Society* 4 (1975): 129–46.

Bonilla-Silva, Eduardo. "The Invisible Weight of Whiteness." *Ethnic and Racial Studies* 35 (2012): 173–94.

Bourdieu, Pierre. *Outline of a Theory of Practice*. New York: Cambridge University Press, 1977 [1972].

———. *Distinction: A Social Critique of the Judgement of Taste*. Cambridge, MA: Harvard University Press, 1984 [1979].

———. *The Logic of Practice*. Palo Alto, CA: Stanford University Press, 1990 [1980].

Brazile, Donna. "Why 'All Lives Matter' Misses the Point." www.cnn.com/2015/07/22/opinions/brazile-black-lives-matter-slogan/.

Brekhus, Wayne H. "Social Marking and the Mental Coloring of Identity: Sexual Identity Construction and Maintenance in the United States." *Sociological Forum* 11 (1996): 497–522.

———. "A Sociology of the Unmarked: Redirecting Our Focus." *Sociological Theory* 16 (1998): 34–51.

———. *Peacocks, Chameleons, Centaurs: Gay Suburbia and the Grammar of Social Identity*. Chicago: University of Chicago Press, 2003.

———. *Culture and Cognition: Patterns in the Social Construction of Reality*. Cambridge, UK: Polity Press, 2015.

Brekhus, Wayne H., et al. "On the Contributions of Cognitive Sociology to the Sociological Study of Race." *Sociology Compass* 4 (2010): 61–76.

Brod, Harry. "The Case for Superordinate Studies." *Transformations* 8.2 (September 30, 1997): 54.

———. "Studying Masculinities as Superordinate Studies." In Judith K. Gardiner (ed.), *Masculinity Studies and Feminist Theory: New Directions*, 161–75. New York: Columbia University Press, 2002.

Brooker, Peter. "Key Words in Brecht's Theory and Practice of Theatre." In Peter Thomson and Glendyr Sacks (eds.), *The Cambridge Companion to*

Brecht, 2nd ed., 209–24. Cambridge, UK: Cambridge University Press, 2006 [1994].

Brown, Tom. "Fill Your Senses, Light Up Your Life." *Reader's Digest*, August 1984, 153–56.

Bruni, Frank. "Do Gays Unsettle You?" *New York Times*, February 8, 2015a, Sunday Review Section, 3.

———. "Hillary's Shelved Crown." *New York Times*, April 19, 2015b, Sunday Review Section, P3.

Bucholtz, Mary. "You da Man: Narrating the Racial Other in the Production of White Masculinity." *Journal of Sociolinguistics* 3 (1999): 443–60.

Bundy, Penny, et al. "Drama and the Audience: Transformative Encounters in TheatreSpace." In Michael Anderson and Julie Dunn (eds.), *How Drama Activates Learning: Contemporary Research and Practice*, 145–58. London: Bloomsbury Academic, 2013.

Butler, Catherine. "An Awareness-Raising Tool Addressing Lesbian and Gay Lives." *Clinical Psychology* 36 (2004): 15–17.

Butler, Samuel. *Life and Habit*. The Floating Press, 2013 [1878].

Caffi, C. "Presupposition, Pragmatic." In Peter V. Lamarque (ed.), *Concise Encyclopedia of Philosophy of Language*, 437–44. Oxford: Pergamon 1997.

Calaprice, Alice (ed.). *The Ultimate Quotable Einstein*. Princeton, NJ: Princeton University Press, 2010.

Canguilhem, Georges. *The Normal and the Pathological*. New York: Zone Books, 1991 [1966].

Carroll, Noël. *The Philosophy of Horror or Paradoxes of the Heart*. New York: Routledge, 1990.

Cerulo, Karen A. *Never Saw It Coming: Cultural Challenges to Envisioning the Worst*. Chicago: University of Chicago Press, 2006.

Chambers, Ross. "The Unexamined." *Minnesota Review* 47 (1996): 141–56.

Chandler, Daniel. *Semiotics: The Basics*. 2nd ed. London: Routledge, 2007.

Chozick, Amy. "Middle Class Is Disappearing, at Least from Vocabulary of Possible 2016 Contenders." *New York Times*, May 12, 2015, A15.

Clark, Herbert H. "Linguistic Processes in Deductive Reasoning." *Psychological Review* 76 (1969): 387–404.

Clark, Herbert H., and Eve V. Clark. *Psychology and Language: An Introduction to Psycholinguistics*. New York: Harcourt Brace Jovanovich, 1977.

Coffey, Amanda. *Reconceptualizing Social Policy: Sociological Perspectives on Contemporary Social Policy*. New York: Open University Press, 2004.

Cohen, Stanley. *Folk Devils and Moral Panics: The Creation of the Mods and Rockers*. London: MacGibbon and Key, 1972.

Cole, Matthew, and Karen Morgan. "Vegaphobia: Derogatory Discourses of Veganism and the Reproduction of Speciesism in UK National Newspapers." *British Journal of Sociology* 62 (2011): 134–53.

Coleridge, Samuel T. *Biographia Literaria: Biographical Sketches of My Literary Life*. Princeton, NJ: Princeton University Press, 1983 [1817].

Collinson, David, and Jeff Hearn. "Naming Men as Men: Implications for Work, Organization, and Management." *Gender, Work, and Organization* 1 (1994): 2–22.

Comrie, Bernard. *Aspect: An Introduction to the Study of Verbal Aspect and Related Problems*. Cambridge, UK: Cambridge University Press, 1976.

Coulter, Ann. "Any Growing Interest in Soccer a Sign of Nation's Moral Decay." *The Clarion-Ledger*, June 26, 2014. http://www.clarionledger.com/story/opinion/columnists/2014/06/25/coulter-growing-interest-soccer-sign-nations-moral-decay/11372137.

Davis, Lennard J. *Enforcing Normalcy: Disability, Deafness, and the Body*. London: Verso, 1995.

Davis, Murray S. *What's So Funny? The Comic Conception of Culture and Society*. Chicago: University of Chicago Press, 1993.

Dean, James J. *Straights: Heterosexuality in Post-Closeted Culture*. New York: New York University Press, 2014.

DeGloma, Thomas. "The Social Logic of 'False Memories': Symbolic Awakenings and Symbolic Worlds in Survivor and Retractor Memories." *Symbolic Interaction* 30 (2007): 543–65.

———. "The Unconscious in Cultural Dispute: On the Ethics of Psychosocial Discovery." In Lynn Chancer and John Andrews (eds.), *The Unhappy Divorce of Sociology and Psychoanalysis: Diverse Perspectives on the Psychosocial*, 77–97. New York: Palgrave Macmillan, 2014.

Deikman, Arthur J. "De-Automatization and the Mystic Experience." *Psychiatry* 29 (1966): 324–38.

Delamont, Sara, and Paul Atkinson. *Fighting Familiarity: Essays on Education and Ethnography*. Cresskill, NJ: Hampton Press, 1995.

Dickinson, Amy. "Ask Amy: Parent Pressures Gay Son to Change." November 12, 2013. https://www.washingtonpost.com/lifestyle/style/ask-amy-parent-pressures-gay-son-to-change/2013/11/12/a46984d0-4815-11e3-bf0c-cebf37c6f484_story.html?utm_term=.7f9f2660267e.

DiMaggio, Paul. "Culture and Cognition." *Annual Review of Sociology* 23 (1997): 263–87.

Dirks, Danielle, and Emily I. Troshynski. "Date and Acquaintance Rape." In Constance L. Shehan (ed.), *The Wiley Blackwell Encyclopedia of Family Studies*, vol. 2, 507–13. Chichester, UK: John Wiley and Sons, 2016.

Dixon, Wheeler W. *Straight: Constructions of Heterosexuality in the Cinema*. Albany: State University of New York Press, 2003.

Doane, Ashley W. Jr. "Dominant Group Ethnic Identity in the United States: The Role of 'Hidden' Ethnicity in Intergroup Relations." *Sociological Quarterly* 38 (1997): 375–97.

———. "Rethinking Whiteness Studies." In Ashley W. Doane and Eduardo Bonilla-Silva (eds.), *White Out: The Continuing Significance of Racism*, 3–18. New York: Routledge, 2003.

Dolmage, Jay, and Cynthia Lewiecki-Wilson. "Refiguring Rhetorica: Linking Feminist Rhetoric and Disability Studies." In Eileen E. Schell and K. J. Rawson (eds.), *Rhetorica in Motion: Feminist Rhetorical Methods and Methodologies*, 23–38. Pittsburgh: University of Pittsburgh Press, 2010.

Dudley-Marling, Curt, and Alex Gurn (eds.). *The Myth of the Normal Curve.* New York: Peter Lang, 2010.

Dunn, Alan. "Average America vs. the One Percent." *Forbes*, March 21, 2012. https://www.forbes.com/sites/moneywisewomen/2012/03/21/average-america-vs-the-one-percent/2/#1050984b1077.

Durkheim, Emile. *The Rules of Sociological Method.* New York: Free Press, 1982 [1895].

———. *The Elementary Forms of Religious Life.* New York: Free Press, 1995 [1912].

———. "The Dualism of Human Nature and Its Social Conditions." In Robert N. Bellah (ed.), *Emile Durkheim: On Morality and Society*, 149–63. Chicago: University of Chicago Press, 1973 [1914].

Dyer, Richard. *White.* London: Routledge, 1997.

Edwards, Betty. *Drawing on the Right Side of the Brain: A Course in Enhancing Creativity and Artistic Confidence.* Los Angeles: J. P. Tarcher, 1979.

———. *The New Drawing on the Right Side of the Brain.* New York: Jeremy P. Tarcher/Putnam, 1999.

Ehrenzweig, Anton. *The Psycho-Analysis of Artistic Vision and Hearing: An Introduction to a Theory of Unconscious Perception.* New York: The Julian Press, 1953.

Eichler, Margrit, et al. "Gender Bias in Medical Research." *Women and Therapy* 12 (1992): 61–70.

Eliason, Michele J. *Who Cares? Institutional Barriers to Health Care for Lesbian, Gay, and Bisexual Persons.* New York: National League for Nursing Press, 1996.

Elšík, Viktor, and Yaron Matras. *Markedness and Language Change: The Romani Sample.* Berlin: Mouton de Gruyter, 2006.

Ergun, Emek. "Bridging across Feminist Translation and Sociolinguistics." *Language and Linguistics Compass* 4 (2010): 307–18.

Erikson, Kai T. *Wayward Puritans: A Study in the Sociology of Deviance.* New York: John Wiley & Sons, 1966.

———. *Everything in Its Path: Destruction of Community in the Buffalo Creek Flood.* New York: Simon and Schuster, 1976.

Eriksson, Stig A. "Distancing." In Shifra Schonmann (ed.), *Key Concepts in Theatre/Drama Education*, 65–71. Rotterdam, The Netherlands: Sense Publishers, 2011.

Fasold, Ralph. *The Sociolinguistics of Language*. Cambridge, MA: Basil Blackwell, 1990.

Fiedler, Leslie. "The Tyranny of the Normal." In *Tyranny of the Normal: Essays on Bioethics, Theology, and Myth*, 147–55. Boston: David R. Godine, 1996 [1984].

Fields, Erica L., and Alisha L. Kirchoff. "Date Rape." In William J. Chambliss (ed.), *Crime and Criminal Behavior*, 71–83. Thousand Oaks, CA: SAGE Publications, 2011.

Fingarette, Herbert. *Self-Deception*. London: Routledge & Kegan Paul, 1969.

Fleck, Ludwik. *Genesis and Development of a Scientific Fact*. Chicago: University of Chicago Press, 1979 [1935].

Force, William R. "The Code of Harry: Performing Normativity in Dexter." *Crime, Media, Culture* 6 (2010): 329–45.

Foster, Johanna. "Menstrual Time: The Sociocognitive Mapping of 'The Menstrual Cycle.'" *Sociological Forum* 11 (1996): 523–47.

Foucault, Michel. *Discipline and Punish: The Birth of the Prison*. New York: Vintage Books, 1979 [1975].

———. *Abnormal: Lectures at the Collège de France 1974–1975*. New York: Picador, 2003 [1975].

Francis, Ara. *Family Trouble: Middle-Class Parents, Children's Problems, and the Disruption of Everyday Life*. New Brunswick, NJ: Rutgers University Press, 2015.

Frank, Francine W., and Paula A. Treichler. *Language, Gender, and Professional Writing: Theoretical Approaches and Guidelines for Nonsexist Usage*. New York: The Modern Language Association of America, 1989.

Frankenberg, Ruth. *White Women, Race Matters: The Social Construction of Whiteness*. Minneapolis: University of Minnesota Press, 1993.

———. "The Mirage of an Unmarked Whiteness." In Birgit B. Rasmussen et al. (eds.), *The Making and Unmaking of Whiteness*, 72–96. Durham, NC: Duke University Press, 2001.

———. "On Unsteady Ground: Crafting and Engaging in the Critical Study of Whiteness." In Martin Bulmer and John Solomos (eds.), *Researching Race and Racism*, 104–18. London: Routledge, 2004.

Friedman, Asia. *Blind to Sameness: Sexpectations and the Social Construction of Male and Female Bodies*. Chicago: University of Chicago Press, 2013.

———. "Cultural Blind Spots and Blind Fields: Collective Forms of Unawareness." In Wayne H. Brekhus and Gabe Ignatow (eds.), *The Oxford Handbook of Cognitive Sociology*. Oxford, UK: Oxford University Press, forthcoming.

Gabriel, John. *Whitewash: Racialized Politics and the Media*. London: Routledge, 1998.

Galotti, Christine. "Correcting Corporeality: Modifying the Body to Privilege the Meadian 'Me.'" Unpublished manuscript, Rutgers University, 2016.

Garfinkel, Harold. "Studies of the Routine Grounds of Everyday Activities." In *Studies in Ethnomethodology*, 35–75. Englewood Cliffs, NJ: Prentice-Hall, 1967 [1964].

Garland-Thomson, Rosemarie. *Extraordinary Bodies: Figuring Physical Disability in American Culture and Literature*. New York: Columbia University Press, 1997.

———. "Integrating Disability, Transforming Feminist Theory." *NWSA Journal* 14.3 (2002): 1–32.

Genieys, William, and Marc Smyrl. *Elites, Ideas, and the Evolution of Public Policy*. New York: Palgrave Macmillan, 2008.

Gervis, Alexandra. "Bringing Forth the Background: Social Movements That Find Power in What We Take for Granted." Paper presented at the annual meeting of the Eastern Sociological Society, New York, February 2015.

Givón, Talmy. *Syntax: A Functional-Typological Introduction, Vol. 2*. Amsterdam: John Benjamins, 1990.

———. *Functionalism and Grammar*. Amsterdam: John Benjamins, 1995.

———. *Syntax: An Introduction, Vol. 1*. Amsterdam: John Benjamins, 2001.

Goffman, Erving. *Behavior in Public Places: Notes on the Social Organization of Gatherings*. New York: Free Press, 1963a.

———. *Stigma: Notes on the Management of Spoiled Identity*. Englewood Cliffs, NJ: Prentice-Hall, 1963b.

———. *Relations in Public: Microstudies of the Public Order*. New York: Basic Books, 1971.

Goldstein, Eric L. *The Price of Whiteness: Jews, Race, and American Identity*. Princeton, NJ: Princeton University Press, 2006.

Gordon, William J. *Synectics: The Development of Creative Capacity*. New York: Harper and Row, 1961.

Graham, Elaine L. *Representations of the Post/Human: Monsters, Aliens, and Others in Popular Culture*. New Brunswick, NJ: Rutgers University Press, 2002.

Gramsci, Antonio. "Science, Humanity, Objectivity." In Derek Boothman (ed.), *Further Selections from the Prison Notebooks*, 290–92. Minneapolis: University of Minnesota Press, 1995.

Grazian, David. *American Zoo: A Sociological Safari*. Princeton, NJ: Princeton University Press, 2015.

Greenberg, Joseph H. *Language Universals: With Special Reference to Feature Hierarchies*. The Hague: Mouton, 1966.

Gronow, Jukka, and Alan Warde. "Introduction." In *Ordinary Consumption*, 1–8. London: Routledge, 2001.

Halfacree, Keith. "Jumping Up from the Armchair: Beyond the Idyll in Counterurbanisation." In Michaela Benson and Nick Osbaldiston (eds.), *Migration, Diasporas, and Citizenship: Theoretical Approaches to Migration and the Quest for a Better Way of Life*, 92–115. Houndmills, UK: Palgrave Macmillan, 2014.

Hall, Edward T. *The Hidden Dimension*. Garden City, NY: Anchor Books, 1969 [1966].

Haraway, Donna J. *Primate Visions: Gender, Race, and Nature in the World of Modern Science*. New York: Routledge, 1989.

Harper, Robyn. "When I Get Married, Will It Be a 'Gay Marriage'?" *Huffington Post*, June 6, 2012. http://www.huffingtonpost.com/robyn-harper /marriage-quality_b_1572611.html.

Harris, Richard J. "Answering Questions Containing Marked and Unmarked Adjectives and Adverbs." *Journal of Experimental Psychology* 97 (1973): 399–401.

Hartigan, John Jr. *Odd Tribes: Toward a Cultural Analysis of White People*. Durham, NC: Duke University Press, 2005.

Haspelmath, Martin. "Against Markedness (and What to Replace It With)." *Journal of Linguistics* 42 (2006): 25–70.

Havránek, Bohuslav. "The Functional Differentiation of the Standard Language." In Paul L. Garvin (ed.), *A Prague School Reader on Esthetics, Literary Structure, and Style*, 3–16. Washington, DC: Georgetown University Press, 1964 [1932].

Hawkes, Terence. *Structuralism and Semiotics*. Berkeley: University of California Press, 1977.

Healy, Patrick, and Michael Barbaro. "Trump Wants to Block Entry of All Muslims." *New York Times*, December 8, 2015, A1, A19.

Heath, Melanie. "Sexual Misgivings: Producing Un/Marked Knowledge in Neoliberal Marriage Promotion Policies." *Sociological Quarterly* 54 (2013): 561–83.

Hegel, Georg W. F. *The Phenomenology of Mind*. Mineola, NY: Dover Publications, 2003 [1807].

Hertz, Robert. "The Pre-eminence of the Right Hand: A Study in Religious Polarity." In Rodney Needham (ed.), *Right and Left: Essays on Dual Symbolic Classification*, 3–22. Chicago: University of Chicago Press, 1973 [1909].

Hockey, Jenny, et al. *Mundane Heterosexualities: From Theory to Practices*. Basingstoke, UK: Palgrave Macmillan, 2007.

Hofmann, Thomas R. *Realms of Meaning: An Introduction to Semantics*. New York: Routledge, 1993.

Hofstadter, Douglas R. "Changes in Default Words and Images, Engendered by Rising Consciousness." In *Metamagical Themas: Questing for the Essence of Mind and Pattern*, 136–58. New York: Basic Books, 1985 [1982].

Holleman, Bregje C., and Henk L. W. Pander Maat. "The Pragmatics of Profiling: Framing Effects in Text Interpretation and Text Production." *Journal of Pragmatics* 41 (2009): 2204–21.

Horowitz, Alexandra. *On Looking: Eleven Walks with Expert Eyes*. New York: Scribner, 2013.

Horowitz, Seth S. "The Science and Art of Listening." *New York Times*, November 11, 2012. http://www.nytimes.com/2012/11/11/opinion/sunday/why-listening-is-so-much-more-than-hearing.html?_r=0 (accessed on April 22, 2013).

Horwitz, Allan V. *What's Normal? Reconciling Biology and Culture*. New York: Oxford University Press, 2016.

Huang, Yan. *The Oxford Dictionary of Pragmatics*. Oxford, UK: Oxford University Press, 2012.

Hundeide, Karsten. "The Tacit Background of Children's Judgments." In James V. Wersch (ed.), *Culture, Communication, and Cognition: Vygotskian Perspectives*, 306–22. Cambridge, UK: Cambridge University Press, 1985.

Ignatiev, Noel. *How the Irish Became White*. New York: Routledge, 1995.

Ingraham, Chrys (ed.). *Thinking Straight: The Power, the Promise, and the Paradox of Heterosexuality*. New York: Routledge, 2005.

Jackson, Stevi. "Sexuality, Heterosexuality, and Gender Hierarchy: Getting Our Priorities Straight." In Chrys Ingraham (ed.), *Thinking Straight: The Power, the Promise, and the Paradox of Heterosexuality*, 15–37. New York: Routledge, 2005.

Jakobson, Roman. "Verbal Communication." *Scientific American* 227 (1972): 72–80.

Jakobson, Roman, and Krystyna Pomorska. *Dialogues*. Cambridge, MA: MIT Press, 1983 [1980].

Jakobson, Roman, and Linda R. Waugh. *The Sound Shape of Language*. 3rd ed. Berlin: Walter de Gruyter, 2002 [1979].

James, William. *Some Problems of Philosophy: A Beginning of an Introduction to Philosophy*. London: Longman, Green, 1911.

Jaszczolt, Katarzyna M. *Default Semantics: Foundations of a Compositional Theory of Acts of Communication*. New York: Oxford University Press, 2005.

Joy, Melanie. *Why We Love Dogs, Eat Pigs, and Wear Cows: An Introduction to Carnism*. San Francisco: Conari Press, 2010.

Kabat-Zinn, Jon. *Full Catastrophe Living: Using the Wisdom of Your Body and Mind to Face Stress, Pain, and Illness*. New York: Delacorte Press, 1990.

Katz, Jonathan N. *The Invention of Heterosexuality*. Chicago: University of Chicago Press, 2007 [1995].

Keller, Hildegard E. *My Secret Is Mine: Studies on Religion and Eros in the German Middle Ages*. Leuven, Belgium: Peeters Publishers, 2000.

Kelly, Liz. *Surviving Sexual Violence*. Minneapolis: University of Minnesota Press, 1988.

Khosroshahi, Fatemeh. "Penguins Don't Care, But Women Do: A Social Identity Analysis of a Whorfian Problem." *Language in Society* 18 (1989): 505–25.

Kiesling, Scott. "Men, Masculinities, and Language." *Language and Linguistics Compass* 1 (2007): 653–73.

Kimmel, Michael, and Gloria Steinem. " 'Yes' Is Better than 'No.' " *New York Times*, September 5, 2014, A27.

Kinsey, Alfred C., et al. *Sexual Behavior in the Human Male*. Bloomington: Indiana University Press, 1948.

Kipling, Rudyard. *From Sea to Sea and Other Sketches: Letters of Travel*. 2 vols. Garden City, NY: Doubleday, Page, 1907.

Kitzinger, Celia. "Heteronormativity in Action: Reproducing the Heterosexual Nuclear Family in After-Hours Medical Calls." *Social Problems* 52 (2005a): 477–98.

———. " 'Speaking as a Heterosexual': (How) Does Sexuality Matter for Talk-in-Interaction?" *Research on Language and Social Interaction* 38 (2005b): 221–65.

Koyama, Emi. " 'Cis' Is Real Even If It Is Carelessly Articulated." eminism.org /blog/entry/399, September 9, 2013 [2002].

Kuhn, Thomas S. *The Structure of Scientific Revolutions*. Chicago: University of Chicago Press, 1970 [1962].

Kuipers, Aert H. "On Symbols, Distinctions and Markedness." *Lingua* 36 (1975): 31–46.

Labov, William. "The Logic of Nonstandard English." In *Language in the Inner City: Studies in the Black English Vernacular*, 201–40. Philadelphia: University of Pennsylvania Press, 1972 [1969].

Lakoff, George. *Women, Fire, and Dangerous Things: What Categories Reveal about the Mind*. Chicago: University of Chicago Press, 1987.

Lander, Christian. *Stuff White People Like: The Definitive Guide to the Unique Taste of Millions*. New York: Random House, 2008.

Larson, Gary. *The Complete Far Side: Volume Two 1987–1994*. Kansas City, MO: Andrews McMeel Publishing, 2003.

Lerner, Adam B. "The Calculus behind Hillary Clinton and 'Everyday Americans.' " April 18, 2015. http://www.politico.com/story/2015/04/the -calculus-behind-hillary-clinton-and-everyday-americans-117099.html.

Levinson, Stephen C. *Presumptive Meanings: The Theory of Generalized Conversational Implicature*. Cambridge, MA: MIT Press, 2000.

Lewis, Andrew R., and Paul A. Djupe. "Where to Say 'Merry Christmas' vs. 'Happy Holidays'—2016 Edition." http://fivethirtyeight.com/features /where-to-say-merry-christmas-vs- happy-holidays-2016-edition/ (accessed on December 23, 2016).

Lieberson, Stanley. "Unhyphenated Whites in the United States." *Ethnic and Racial Studies* 8 (1985): 159–80.

Linton, Simi. *Claiming Disability: Knowledge and Identity*. New York: New York University Press, 1998.

Lippi-Green, Rosina. *English with an Accent: Language, Ideology, and Discrimination in the United States*. London: Routledge, 1997.

Livia, Anna. *Pronoun Envy: Literary Uses of Linguistic Gender*. New York: Oxford University Press, 2001.

Lyons, John. *Semantics, Vol.1*. Cambridge, UK: Cambridge University Press, 1977.

MacCannell, Dean. *The Tourist: A New Theory of the Leisure Class*. Berkeley: University of California Press, 1999 [1976].

MacKinnon, Catharine A. *Sexual Harassment of Working Women: A Case of Sexual Discrimination*. New Haven, CT: Yale University Press, 1979.

Mahler, Jonathan. "In Campaign and Company, Daughter Has a Central Role." *New York Times*, April 17, 2016, A1, A18.

Manning, Susan. "Danced Spirituals." In André Lepecki (ed.), *Of the Presence of the Body: Essays on Dance and Performance Theory*, 82–96. Middletown, CT: Wesleyan University Press, 2004.

Martella, Giuseppe. "From Index to Link: A Phenomenology of Language." In Martin Procházka et al. (eds.), *The Prague School and Theories of Structure*, 427–36. Göttingen, Germany: V & R Unipress, 2010.

Martin, Karin A. "Normalizing Heterosexuality: Mothers' Assumptions, Talk, and Strategies with Young Children." *American Sociological Review* 74 (2009): 190–207.

Martyna, Wendy. "Beyond the 'He/Man' Approach: The Case for Nonsexist Language." *Signs* 5 (1980): 482–93.

Matsuda, Mari J. "Voices of America: Accent, Antidiscrimination Law, and a Jurisprudence for the Last Reconstruction." *Yale Law Journal* 100 (1991): 1329–407.

Maugham, W. Somerset. *Of Human Bondage*. New York: Grosset and Dunlap, 1915.

McDermott, Monica, and Frank L. Samson. "White Racial and Ethnic Identity in the United States." *Annual Review of Sociology* 31 (2005): 245–61.

McGill, Andrew. "Merry Christmas vs. Happy Holidays, Round 2,016: The Perennial Debate Gets a New Coat of Cheers from Donald Trump." *The Atlantic*, December 20, 2016. https://www.theatlantic.com/politics/archive/2016/12/merry-christmas-vs-happy-holidays-round-2016/511115/.

McIntosh, Peggy. "White Privilege: Unpacking the Invisible Knapsack." *Peace and Freedom Magazine*, July/August 1989, 10–12.

McRuer, Robert. *Crip Theory: Cultural Signs of Queerness and Disability*. New York: New York University Press, 2006.

Miall, David S., and Don Kuiken. "Foregrounding, Defamiliarization, and Affect: Response to Literary Stories." *Poetics* 22 (1994): 389–407.

Micciche, Laura R. "Writing as Feminist Rhetorical Theory." In Eileen E. Schell and Kelly J. Rawson (eds.), *Rhetorica in Motion: Feminist Rhetorical Methods and Methodologies*, 173–88. Pittsburgh, PA: University of Pittsburgh Press, 2010.

Milgram, Stanley. "On Maintaining Social Norms: A Field Experiment in the Subway." In *The Individual in a Social World: Essays and Experiments*, 37–46. New York: McGraw-Hill, 1992 [1978].

Millar, Robert M., and Robert L. Trask. *Trask's Historical Linguistics*. 3rd ed. New York: Routledge, 2015.

Miller, Daniel, and Sophie Woodward. *Blue Jeans: The Art of the Ordinary*. Berkeley: University of California Press, 2012.

Miner, Horace. "Body Ritual among the Nacirema." *American Anthropologist* 58 (1956): 503–07.

Minnich, Elizabeth K. *Transforming Knowledge*. 2nd ed. Philadelphia: Temple University Press, 2005.

Misztal, Barbara A. "Normality and Trust in Goffman's Theory of Interaction Order." *Sociological Theory* 19 (2001): 312–24.

———. *Multiple Normalities: Making Sense of Ways of Living*. New York: Palgrave Macmillan, 2015.

Moore, Robert B. "Racism in the English Language." In Jodi O'Brien (ed.), *The Production of Reality: Essays and Readings on Social Interaction*, 4th ed., 119–26. Thousand Oaks, CA: Pine Forge Press, 2005 [1976].

Moore, Valerie A. "The Collaborative Emergence of Race in Children's Play: A Case Study of Two Summer Camps." *Social Problems* 49 (2002): 58–78.

Morin, Stephen F., and Douglas C. Kimmel. "Martin Rochlin (1928–2003)." *American Psychologist* 59 (2004): 958.

Morris, Charles. "Foundations of the Theory of Signs." In *Writings on the General Theory of Signs*, 13–71. The Hague: Mouton, 1971 [1938].

Morris, Wayne. "Transforming Able-Bodied Normativity: The Wounded Christ and Human Vulnerability." *Irish Theological Quarterly* 78 (2013): 231–43.

Moser, Charles, and Peggy Kleinplatz. "Does Heterosexuality Belong in the DSM?" *Lesbian & Gay Psychology Review* 6 (2005): 261–67.

Motschenbacher, Heiko. *Language, Gender, and Sexual Identity: Poststructural Perspectives*. Amsterdam: John Benjamins, 2010.

Mukařovský, Jan. "Standard Language and Poetic Language." In Paul L. Garvin (ed.), *A Prague School Reader on Esthetics, Literary Structure, and Style*, 17–30. Washington, DC: Georgetown University Press, 1964 [1932].

Mullaney, Jamie L. "Making It 'Count': Mental Weighing and Identity Attribution." *Symbolic Interaction* 22 (1999): 269–83.

———. *Everyone Is NOT Doing It: Abstinence and Personal Identity*. Chicago: University of Chicago Press, 2006.

Murphy, Lauren. "Large but Not in Charge: A Sociocognitive Approach to Fat Invisibility in the Media." Unpublished manuscript, Rutgers University, Department of Sociology, 2011.

Myers, Robert. "The Familiar Strange and the Strange Familiar in Anthropology and Beyond." *General Anthropology* 18.2 (2011): 1–9.

Ndopu, Eddie. "Able Normative Supremacy and the Zero Mentality." *The Feminist Wire*, February 5, 2013. http://www.thefeministwire.com/2013/02/able-normative-supremacy-and-the-zero-mentality/ (accessed on July 19, 2015).

Newfield, Madeleine, and Linda R. Waugh. "Invariance and Markedness in Grammatical Categories." In Linda R. Waugh and Stephen Rudy (eds.), *New Vistas in Grammar: Invariance and Variation*, 221–38. Amsterdam: John Benjamins, 1991 [1985].

Nietzsche, Friedrich. *The Gay Science: With a Prelude in Rhymes and an Appendix of Songs*. New York: Vintage Books, 1974 [1887].

O'Brien, William A. *Novalis: Signs of Revolution*. Durham, NC: Duke University Press, 1995.

Olick, Jeffrey K., et al. "Response to Our Critics." *Memory Studies* 7 (2014): 131–38.

Ornstein, Robert. *Meditation and Modern Psychology*. Los Altos, CA: Malor Books, 2008 [1971].

Ostrow, James M. *Social Sensitivity: A Study of Habit and Experience*. Albany: State University of New York Press, 1990.

Otto, Hiltrud, et al. "Cultural Differences in Stranger-Child Interactions: A Comparison between German Middle-Class and Cameroonian Nso Stranger-Infant Dyad." *Journal of Cross-Cultural Psychology* 45 (2014): 322–34.

Pagliai, Valentina. "Unmarked Racializing Discourse, Facework, and Identity in Talk about Immigrants in Italy." *Journal of Linguistic Anthropology* 21 (2011): E94–E112.

Perec, Georges. "Approaches to What?" In *Species of Spaces and Other Pieces*, 205–7. London: Penguin Books, 1997 [1973].

———. *An Attempt at Exhausting a Place in Paris*. Cambridge, MA: Wakefield Press, 1975.

Perry, Pamela. "White Means Never Having to Say You're Ethnic: White Youth and the Construction of 'Cultureless' Identities." *Journal of Contemporary Ethnography* 30 (2001): 56–91.

———. *Shades of White: White Kids and Racial Identities in High School*. Durham, NC: Duke University Press, 2002.

Petulla, Sam. "'Merry Christmas' versus 'Happy Holidays': Why Trump May Prefer the Former." *NBC News*, December 24, 2016. http://www.nbcnews.com/news/us-news/merry-christmas-versus-happy-holidays-why-trump-prefers-former-n699611.

Polanyi, Michael. *The Tacit Dimension*. Chicago: University of Chicago Press, 1966.

Poovey, Mary. "Sex in America." *Critical Inquiry* 24 (1998): 366–92.

Proust, Marcel. *Remembrance of Things Past, Vol. 2*. Hertfordshire, UK: Wordworth Editions, 2006 [1923].

Purcell, Carl. *Your Artist's Brain*. Cincinnati: North Light Books, 2010.

Quetelet, Adolphe. *A Treatise on Man and the Development of His Faculties.* Edinburgh: William and Robert Chambers, 1842 [1835].

Reynolds, David J., et al. "Evidence of Immediate Activation of Gender Information from a Social Role Name." *Quarterly Journal of Experimental Psychology* 59 (2006): 886–903.

Rich, Adrienne. "Compulsory Heterosexuality and Lesbian Existence." *Signs* 5 (1980): 631–60.

Robinson, Douglas. *Estrangement and the Somatics of Literature: Tolstoy, Shklovsky, Brecht.* Baltimore: Johns Hopkins University Press, 2008.

Robinson, Sally. *Marked Men: White Masculinity in Crisis.* New York: Columbia University Press, 2000.

Rochlin, Martin. "Heterosexual Questionnaire." https://www.uwgb.edu/pride-center/files/pdfs/Heterosexual_Questionnaire.pdf (accessed on June 27, 2015).

Roediger, David R. *Working toward Whiteness: How America's Immigrants Became White.* New York: Basic Books, 2005.

Rogers, Mary F. "Taken-for-Grantedness." *Current Perspectives in Social Theory* 2 (1981): 133–51.

Romaine, Suzanne. *Communicating Gender.* Mahwah, NJ: Lawrence Erlbaum, 1999.

Rothblum, Esther. "Poly-Friendships." *Journal of Lesbian Studies* 3 (1999): 71–83.

Rubin, Gayle S. "Thinking Sex: Notes for a Radical Theory of the Politics of Sexuality." In Ken Plummer (ed.), *Sexualities: Critical Concepts in Sociology,* 188–241. New York: Routledge, 2002 [1984].

Ryan, Dan. "Getting the Word Out: Notes on the Social Organization of Notification." *Sociological Theory* 24 (2006): 228–54.

Ryder, Richard D. *Animal Revolution: Changing Attitudes towards Speciesism.* Oxford: Basil Blackwell, 1989.

Safire, William. "On Language: Retronym Watch." *New York Times Magazine,* November 1, 1992. www.nytimes.com/1992/11/01/magazine/on-language-retronym-watch.html.

Said, Edward W. *Orientalism.* New York: Vintage Books, 1979.

Sasson-Levy, Orna. "A Different Kind of Whiteness: Marking and Unmarking of Social Boundaries in the Construction of Hegemonic Ethnicity." *Sociological Forum* 28 (2013): 27–50.

Sasson-Levy, Orna, and Avi Shoshana. "'Passing' as (Non)Ethnic: The Israeli Version of Acting White." *Sociological Inquiry* 83 (2013): 448–72.

Sbisà, Marina. "Ideology and the Persuasive Use of Presupposition." In J. Verschueren (ed.), *Language and Ideology: Selected Papers from the 6th International Pragmatics Conference, Vol. 1,* 492–509. Antwerp, Belgium: International Pragmatics Association, 1999.

Schutz, Alfred. *The Phenomenology of the Social World*. Evanston, IL: North-western University Press, 1967 [1932].

———. "The Well-Informed Citizen: An Essay on the Social Distribution of Knowledge." In *Collected Papers, Vol. II: Studies in Social Theory*, 120–34. The Hague: Martinus Nijhoff, 1964 [1946].

———. "Choosing among Projects of Action." In *Collected Papers, Vol. I: The Problem of Social Reality*, 67–96. The Hague: Martinus Nijhoff, 1973 [1951].

———. "Symbol, Reality, and Society." In *Collected Papers, Vol. I: The Problem of Social Reality*, 287–356. The Hague: Martinus Nijhoff, 1973 [1955].

Schutz, Alfred, and Thomas Luckmann. *The Structures of the Life-World*. Evanston, IL: Northwestern University Press, 1973.

Seymour-Smith, Sarah. "Qualitative Methods." In Christina Richards and Meg J. Barker (eds.), *The Palgrave Handbook of the Psychology of Sexuality and Gender*, 316–32. New York: Palgrave Macmillan, 2015.

Shapiro, Judith. "'Women's Studies': A Note on the Perils of Markedness." *Signs* 7 (1982): 717–21.

Shapiro, Michael. *The Sense of Grammar: Language as Semeiotic*. Bloomington: Indiana University Press, 1983.

Shelley, Percy B. "A Defence of Poetry." In *Essays, Letters from Abroad: Translations and Fragments, Vol.1*, 25–62. Philadelphia: Lea and Blanchard, 1840.

Shepard, Paul. *Thinking Animals: Animals and the Development of Human Intelligence*. New York: Viking Press, 1978.

Shepelak, Norma J. "Neanderthal Person Revisited." *American Sociologist* 11 (1976): 90–92.

Shklovsky, Viktor. "Art as Technique." In Lee T. Lemon and Marion J. Reis (eds.), *Russian Formalist Criticism: Four Essays*, 5–24. Lincoln: University of Nebraska Press, 1965 [1917].

Silveira, Jeanette. "Generic Masculine Words and Thinking." *Women's Studies International Quarterly* 3 (1980): 165–78.

Simon-Vandenbergen, Anne-Marie, et al. "Presupposition and 'Taking-for-Granted' in Mass Communicated Political Argument: An Illustration from British, Flemish, and Swedish Political Colloquy." In Anita Fetzer and Gerda E. Lauerbach (eds.), *Political Discourse in the Media: Cross-Cultural Perspectives*, 31–74. Amsterdam: John Benjamins, 2007.

Simpson, Ruth. "Neither Clear Nor Present: The Social Construction of Safety and Danger." *Sociological Forum* 11 (1996): 549–62.

Simpson, Ruth, and Patricia Lewis. "An Investigation of Silence and a Scrutiny of Transparency: Re-Examining Gender in Organization Literature through the Concepts of Voice and Visibility." *Human Relations* 58 (2005): 1253–75.

Spence, Larry D. *The Politics of Social Knowledge*. University Park: Pennsylvania State University Press, 1978.

Spivak, Gayatri C. "The Rani of Sirmur: An Essay in Reading the Archives." *History and Theory* 24 (1985): 247–72.

Stack, Liam. "How the 'War on Christmas' Controversy Was Created." *New York Times*, December 19, 2016. http://www.nytimes.com/2016/12/19/us /war-on-christmas-controversy.html?_r=0.

Stalnaker, Robert. "Presuppositions." *Journal of Philosophical Logic* 2 (1973): 447–57.

Steinmetz, Katy. "This Is What 'Cisgender' Means." *Time* Magazine, December 23, 2014. time.com/363430/cisgender-definition/.

Stephens, Bret. "Only Mass Deportation Can Save America." *New York Times*, June 16, 2017. https://www.nytimes.com/2017/06/16/opinion/only-mass -deportation-can-save-america.html.

Stoppard, Tom. *Rosencrantz and Guildenstern Are Dead*. New York: Samuel French, 1967.

Strong, Pauline T., and Barrik Van Winkle. "'Indian Blood': Reflections on the Reckoning and Refiguring of Native North American Identity." *Cultural Anthropology* 11 (1996): 547–76.

Surk, Barbara. "Serbia's First Openly Gay Premier Takes On the Insults." *New York Times*, June 29, 2017, A11.

Tajfel, Henri. "The Social Psychology of Minorities." In *Human Groups and Social Categories: Studies in Social Psychology*, 309–43. Cambridge, UK: Cambridge University Press, 1981 [1978].

Tannen, Deborah. "Marked Women, Unmarked Men." *The New York Times Magazine*, June 20, 1993, pp. 18, 52, 54.

Tavory, Iddo, and Stefan Timmermans. *Abductive Analysis: Theorizing Qualitative Research*. Chicago: University of Chicago Press, 2014.

Tavris, Carol. *The Mismeasure of Woman: Why Women Are Not the Better Sex, the Inferior Sex, or the Opposite Sex*. New York: Simon and Schuster, 1992.

Tcholakian, Danielle. "Cuomo Launches Awareness Campaign to Fight Sexual Assault on Campus." *DNA info*, September 2, 2015. http://www.dnainfo .com/new-york/20150902/greenwich-village/cuomo-launches-awareness -campaign-fight-sexual-assault-on-campus.

Terry, Robert W. "The Negative Impact of White Values." In Benjamin P. Bowser and Raymond G. Hunt (eds.), *Impacts of Racism on White Americans*, 119–51. Beverly Hills, CA: SAGE Publications, 1981.

Tin, Louis-Georges. *The Invention of Heterosexual Culture*. Cambridge, MA: MIT Press, 2012 [2008].

Titchkosky, Tanya. *Disability, Self, and Society*. Toronto: University of Toronto Press, 2003.

———. "Disability Studies: The Old and the New." In Rod Michalko and Tanya Titchkosky (eds.), *Rethinking Normalcy: A Disability Studies Reader*, 38–62. Toronto: Canadian Scholars' Press, 2009.

Trechter, Sara, and Mary Bucholtz. "White Noise: Bringing Language into Whiteness Studies." *Journal of Linguistic Anthropology* 11 (2001): 3–21.

Trubetzkoy, Nikolai S. *Principles of Phonology.* Berkeley: University of California Press, 1969 [1939].

———. "On the Development of the Gutturals in the Slavic Languages." In Anatoly Liberman (ed.), *N. S. Trubetzkoy: Studies in General Linguistics and Language Structure,* 157–64. Durham, NC: Duke University Press, 2001.

Tuan, Mia. *Forever Foreigners or Honorary Whites? The Asian Ethnic Experience Today.* New Brunswick, NJ: Rutgers University Press, 1999.

Turner, Stephen P. *Understanding the Tacit.* New York: Routledge, 2014.

Twain, Mark. *The Adventures of Huckleberry Finn.* New York: W. W. Norton, 1961 [1885].

Urciuoli, Bonnie. *Exposing Prejudice: Puerto Rican Experiences of Language, Race, and Class.* Boulder, CO: Westview Press, 1996.

———. "Discussion Essay: Semiotic Properties of Racializing Discourses." *Journal of Linguistic Anthropology* 21 (2011): E113–E22.

Van Peer, Willie. *Stylistics and Psychology: Investigations of Foregrounding.* London: Croom Helm, 1986.

Warner, Michael. "Introduction: Fear of a Queer Planet." *Social Text* 29 (1991): 3–17.

———. *The Trouble with Normal: Sex, Politics, and the Ethics of Queer Life.* Cambridge, MA: Harvard University Press, 1999.

Waters, Mary C. *Ethnic Options: Choosing Identities in America.* Berkeley: University of California Press, 1990.

Waugh, Linda R. *Roman Jakobson's Science of Language.* Lisse, The Netherlands: Peter de Rieder, 1976.

———. "Marked and Unmarked: A Choice between Unequals in Semiotic Structure." *Semiotica* 38 (1982): 299–318.

Weber, Bruce. "Leslie Feinberg, 65, Writer and Activist for Transgender Causes." *New York Times,* November 30, 2014, p. 34.

Wells, Herbert G. "The Country of the Blind." In *Selected Short Stories,* 123–46. Harmondsworth, UK: Penguin Books, 1978 [1904].

Whitehead, Evelyn E., and James D. Whitehead. *Fruitful Embraces: Sexuality, Love, and Justice.* Bloomington, IN: iUniverse, 2014.

Whorf, Benjamin L. "Science and Linguistics." In John B. Carroll (ed.), *Language, Thought, and Reality: Selected Writings of Benjamin Lee Whorf,* 207–19. Cambridge, MA: MIT Press, 1956 [1940].

Whyte, Susan R., and Benedicte Ingstad. "Disability and Culture: An Overview." In Benedicte Ingstad and Susan R. Whyte (eds.), *Disability and Culture,* 3–32. Berkeley: University of California Press, 1995.

Wilkinson, Sue, and Celia Kitzinger (eds.). *Heterosexuality: A Feminism & Psychology Reader.* London: SAGE Publications, 1993.

Willett, John (ed.). *Brecht on Theatre: The Development of an Aesthetic*. New York: Hill and Wang, 1992.

Williams, Serena. "We Must Continue to Dream Big." November 29, 2016. https://www.theguardian.com/lifeandstyle/2016/nov/29/dream-big-open -letter-serena-williams-porter-magazine-incredible-women-of-2016-issue -women-athletes.

Wise, Tim. "Blinded by the White: Race, Crime, and Columbine High." June 1999. www.timwise.org/1999/06/blinded-by-the-white-race-crime-and -columbine-high/.

Witkowski, Stanley R., and Cecil H. Brown. "Marking-Reversals and Cultural Importance." *Language* 59 (1983): 569–82.

Wojcik, Filip. "Signifying Love: The Difference between Platonic and Romantic." Unpublished paper, Rutgers University, Department of Sociology, 2015.

Wouters, Cas. "Changes in the 'Lust Balance' of Sex and Love since the Sexual Revolution." In Ken Plummer (ed.), *Sexualities: Critical Concepts in Sociology*, 37–59. New York: Routledge, 2002 (1998).

Wray, Matt. *Not Quite White: White Trash and the Boundaries of Whiteness*. Durham, NC: Duke University Press, 2006.

Yancy, George, and Judith Butler. "What's Wrong with 'All Lives Matter'?" January 12, 2015. http://opinionator.blogs.nytimes.com/2015/01/12/whats -wrong-with-all-lives-matter/?_r=0.

Ybema, Sierk, and Frans Kamsteeg. "Making the Familiar Strange: A Case for Disengaged Organizational Ethnography." In Sierk Ybema et al. (eds.), *Organizational Ethnography: Studying the Complexities of Everyday Life*, 101–19. London: SAGE Publications, 2009.

Zakia, Richard D. *Perception and Imaging*. 2nd ed. Boston: Focal Press, 2002.

Zelizer, Viviana A. "Payments and Social Ties." *Sociological Forum* 11 (1996): 481–95.

Zerubavel, Eviatar. "If Simmel Were a Fieldworker: On Formal Sociological Theory and Analytical Field Research." *Symbolic Interaction* 3.2 (1980): 25–33.

———. *Hidden Rhythms: Schedules and Calendars in Social Life*. Berkeley: University of California Press, 1985 [1981].

———. *The Seven-Day Circle: The History and Meaning of the Week*. Chicago: University of Chicago Press, 1989 [1985].

———. *Social Mindscapes: An Invitation to Cognitive Sociology*. Cambridge, MA: Harvard University Press, 1997.

———. *Time Maps: Collective Memory and the Social Shape of the Past*. Chicago: University of Chicago Press, 2003.

———. "The Social Marking of the Past: Toward a Socio-Semiotics of Memory." In Roger Friedland and John Mohr (eds.), *Matters of Culture: Cultural Sociology in Practice*, 184–95. Cambridge: Cambridge University Press, 2004.

———. *The Elephant in the Room: Silence and Denial in Everyday Life*. New York: Oxford University Press, 2006.

———. "Generally Speaking: The Logic and Mechanics of Social Pattern Analysis." *Sociological Forum* 22 (2007): 131–45.

———. *Ancestors and Relatives: Genealogy, Identity, and Community*. New York: Oxford University Press, 2011.

———. *Hidden in Plain Sight: The Social Structure of Irrelevance*. New York: Oxford University Press, 2015.

———. "The Five Pillars of Essentialism: Reification and the Social Construction of Objective Reality." *Cultural Sociology* 10 (2016): 69–76.

———. "Cognitive Sociology: Between the Personal and the Universal Mind." In Wayne H. Brekhus and Gabe Ignatow (eds.), *The Oxford Handbook of Cognitive Sociology*. Oxford, UK: Oxford University Press, forthcoming.

Zerubavel, Yael. *Recovered Roots: Collective Memory and the Making of Israeli National Tradition*. Chicago: University of Chicago Press, 1995.

Zhou, Min. "Are Asian Americans Becoming 'White'?" *Contexts* 3.1 (2004): 29–37.

Author Index

Subject Index